books designed with giving in mind

Kid's Pets Book	The Compleat American Housewife 1776	Working Couples
Make It Ahead French Cooking	Low Carbohydrate Cookbook	Mexican
Soups & Stews	Kid's Cookbook	Sunday Breakfast
Crepes & Omelets	Italian	Fisherman's Wharf Cookbook
Microwave Cooking	Cheese Guide & Cookbook	Charcoal Cookbook
Vegetable Cookbook	Miller's German	Ice Cream Cookbook
Kid's Arts and Crafts	Quiche & Souffle	Hippo Hamburger
Bread Baking	To My Daughter, With Love	Blender Cookbook
The Crockery Pot Cookbook	Natural Foods	The Wok, a Chinese Cookbook
Kid's Garden Book	Chinese Vegetarian	Cast Iron Cookbook
Classic Greek Cooking	Jewish Gourmet	Japanese Country
		Fondue Cookbook

from nitty gritty productions

This one is for David,
all by himself.

MAKE IT AHEAD
FRENCH
COOKING

by Paul Mayer

Illustrated by Mike Nelson

© Copyright 1976
Nitty Gritty Productions
Concord, California

A Nitty Gritty Book*
Published by
Nitty Gritty Productions
P.O. Box 5457
Concord, California 94524

*Nitty Gritty Books—Trademark
Owned by Nitty Gritty Productions
Concord, California

ISBN 0-911954-38-4

Library of Congress Cataloging in Publication Data

Mayer, Paul, 1924-
    Make it ahead French cooking.

    Includes index.
    1. Cookery, French. I. Title. II.   Title:
French cooking.
TX719.M394   641.5'944   76-28951
ISBN 0-911954-38-4

TABLE OF CONTENTS

PREFACE

The Tudor Queen of England, Mary, despite the excesses of religious fervor and persecution which earned her the title of "Bloody Mary," is nevertheless, reported to have felt nothing so keenly during her years as England's queen as the loss of the continental port of Calais to the French. It is said Queen Mary once remarked that if they were to cut her open upon her death they would find the word "Calais" engraved upon her heart.

In the 25 years during which I have been conducting cooking classes, I have had one question asked me so repeatedly by my students, I am equally sure if my own heart were laid bare I would find that very question etched there even more deeply than the name of that strategic French port was engraved upon the sovereign's.

"Can I make it ahead?" I wish I had a nickel for everytime I've heard that phrase.

It is, of course, impossible to prepare a fine meal without setting foot in the kitchen, but as the years have passed, and households have become cookless and waitressless, it has become increasingly apparent that if one wishes to entertain at home one must get it all together alone and unaided, at least until dinner time.

Today's hostess must not only prepare for her dinner party, but in between time must cart the kids to school, set the table, arrange the flowers, go to the market, finish the laundry and glamorize herself, along with all of the other things which take up her day. And yet, in spite of it all, she still wishes to prepare a splendid meal for her guests, and I applaud her persistence in so doing.

This volume is an attempt to help make the preparation of some of the more exciting and perhaps previously seemingly complicated dishes a bit easier to prepare.

Everyone knows that casseroles, salads and cold desserts can be made in advance and held until needed, and I have included some of these in the pages which follow. However, I have also taken a look at more traditional recipes and divided their preparation into several parts so that the busy homemaker can prepare them, if not in their entirety, at least to some point at which the dish can be set aside, and continued again closer to dinner time, without harming the final outcome of the recipe. In many cases, all parts of the dish can be completed entirely in advance. Read the instructions carefully before starting because in some instances more time is needed to complete the assembly than in others. It is very easy, having checked out the necessary supplies, to begin a dish only to find that there is not enough time to complete it successfully in time for dinner.

The most tedious and time consuming jobs in the kitchen are those which involve peeling, shredding, chopping or other chores prior to actually putting pot to stove. By getting these tiresome chores out of the way early, there will be more time later for the tasks attendant to getting ready for company.

To further simplify time saving procedures and conserve space, I am including on the next two pages the instructions for two basic items which are referred to many times in various recipes throughout this book. Their page numbers are given each time they appear.

I hope the recipes in this book will prove intriguing, and that their preparation will be made simpler by this method of presentation. Bon Chance and Bon Appetit!

CREME FRAICHE
Fresh Cream

Fresh cream as it appears in French markets is so rich and thick with butterfat it will thicken all by itself. In the United States we are not so fortunate, but we can make an excellent substitute. However, it does not thicken the same and small amounts of potato flour must be added to help it. The necessary amount is indicated in each recipe.

1 pt. whipping cream
1/2 pt. sour cream

With a wire whisk, mix the two creams together in a saucepan. Place over moderate heat until the chill has barely left the mixture and it is lukewarm. Pour into a bowl. Leave un-covered overnight in the refrigerator. It will keep at least a week in a covered container. Makes 2-1/2 to 3 cups.

Creme fraiche and my 7-minute method for cooking green vegetables are used in many recipes in this book, and are presented here for easy reference.

The Paul Mayer Method for Cooking Green Vegetables.

My 7 minute method for cooking fresh peas, green beans, asparagus, broccoli and Brussels sprouts produces delicious vegetables which retain their bright green color.

Bring a teakettle of water to a full boil.

Into another pot with a lid, scatter a little sugar and 1 teaspoon salt. Place over high heat until sugar begins to caramelize.

Quickly add prepared vegetables. Without reducing heat, pour in boiling water. The sugar makes the pan so hot the water never ceases boiling, and the vegetables start cooking immediately. Cover pot and boil rapidly for exactly 7 minutes.

Immediately drain into a colander and rinse briefly with cool tap water to stop the cooking action. The vegetables will remain hot! Drain well.

HOR D'OEUVRES

We live today in the world of the cocktail party complete with trays and trays of finger food, and although the proper designation for such food is "canape," it has become common for these tidbits to be known as hors d'oeuvres.

However, although all canapes are hors d'oeuvres, not all hor d'oeuvres are canapes. Hors d'oeuvres is actually "first course" and the ones offered here are just that. You will also find, further on, a section on salads, many of which could also be classified as first courses, and which would make excellent beginnings for any meal. And, because it's too extra special to leave out, I have slipped a rum-fruit cocktail into this section.

I was told recently by a French restaurateur that he considers the most significant portions of a meal to be the beginning, the cheeses and the dessert. Although I feel that a meal must be considered as an entity, I cannot help but agree that first and final impressions are tremendously important. The hors d'oeuvre is the opening gun, and if you can dazzle your guests straight off, they will proceed to succeeding courses with pleasure and anticipation.

CHAMPIGNONS MARINES
Marinated Mushrooms

1-1/2 lbs. mushrooms
2 lemons
1 onion, finely chopped
6 tbs. Chablis wine
1 tbs. wine vinegar
3 tbs. oil
4 tsp. chopped parsley
salt and pepper
12 small tomato wedges

8

The day before, wash and slice mushrooms. Cook 2 minutes in boiling, salted water to which the juice of 1 lemon has been added. Drain mushrooms and place in a bowl with chopped onion, juice of 1 lemon, Chablis, vinegar, oil, parsley, salt and pepper. Marinate in the refrigerator until needed, (at least 3 hours).

Just before serving time, arrange marinated mushrooms on lettuce leaves and garnish with tomato wedges. Makes 6 servings.

TARTINES DU FROMAGE
Toasted Cheese Squares

Early
in the
day

6 slices firm white bread
4 tbs. butter
1 lb. Philadelphia cream cheese
2 tbs. red wine vinegar
1 whole pimiento, finely chopped
1/2 green pepper
salt and pepper

9

Early in the day, trim crusts from bread. Cut each slice into 4 pieces, making 24 squares. Melt butter and lightly dip both sides of each square into butter. Place on cookie sheet and set aside. Beat cheese until smooth. Blend in vinegar. Finely chop pimiento. Seed and chop green pepper. Add to cream cheese. Season with salt and pepper. Cover and refrigerate.

About 15 minutes before serving time, preheat oven to 450°F. Place buttered toast in the oven and bake until lightly browned, about 5 minutes. Remove from oven and allow to cool slightly. Spread toast squares with cheese mixture, piling it high. Bake 5 minutes or until lightly browned. Serve at once.

FONDUS AU PARMESAN
Deep Fried Cheese Squares

6 tbs. butter
1/2 cup flour
2 cups milk
6 egg yolks
4 ozs. grated Parmesan
salt and pepper
2 eggs, beaten
1 tsp. water
bread crumbs
deep fat for frying

10

Early in the day, melt butter in saucepan. Add flour and cook, stirring, over gentle heat 5 minutes. Add milk gradually, stirring constantly. Bring to a boil and cook 30 minutes over lowest heat. Stir frequently with a wire whisk. Remove from heat and beat in egg yolks and Parmesan. Season with salt and pepper. Spread mixture onto lightly greased metal cake pan. Cover with plastic wrap pressed firmly against the surface to prevent a skin from forming. Refrigerate until needed. **Two hours before serving,** dip pan briefly into hot water to loosen mixture. Turn out onto a heavily floured surface. Using a floured knife, cut mixture into 2-inch squares. Dip pieces in flour then in eggs, which have been combined with 1 teaspoon water. Toss pieces in bread crumbs until thoroughly coated. Refrigerate.

    Just before serving time, heat deep fat to 350°F. Fry the crumb-coated fondus until crisp and golden brown. Drain on absorbent paper and serve while hot. Makes 6 servings.

BOUCHEES A L'OIGNON
Onion Puffs

1 pkg. Pepperidge Farm patty shells
2 tbs. butter
1 small onion, finely chopped
salt and pepper
1 egg
1 tsp. water

12

Early in the day, open the package of patty shells. Place shells separately on the counter to start thawing. Melt butter in a small skillet. Add onion and season highly with salt and pepper. Cook gently until all the moisture has cooked away and the onion is soft and buttery. Spread on a metal plate and chill in the freezer. Beat egg with water. Set aside. Place three of the softened patty shells one on top of the other. Press them down to make 1 piece of smooth flat dough. Roll out on a floured surface until they are thin and will fit onto a 10- x 15-inch cookie sheet. Paint the surface of the pastry with beaten egg. Using a small fluted cutter (diamond shaped is best) mark, but do not cut through, 24 pieces. Place a small amount of the chilled filling in the center of each marked area. Press the remaining 3 patty shells together the same as the first. Roll out another sheet the same size, or a little larger, than the first. Place in position over the filling. Press down thoroughly all around the small mounds of filling. Now, using the same fluted cutter, cut through the pastry so that the mounds of filling are in the center of each piece. Pull away the excess dough and repeat, if desired, until all has been used. With a knife make a steam vent in the center of each bouchee. Paint the surface with beaten egg. Chill or freeze at this point until needed.

About 15 minutes before serving time, bake the bouchees in 400°F. oven 10 to 15 minutes or until they have puffed and browned. Serve hot. Makes 6 to 8 servings.

PATE DE CANARD MAISON
Duck Pate

One day ahead

2 ducks (4-6 lbs. ea.)
10 ozs. lean veal
5 ozs. pork filet
1 lb. fresh pork fat
2 eggs, beaten
3 tbs. creme fraiche, page 4

1 tbs. port wine
1 tbs. dark rum
salt and pepper
1/4 lb. baked ham
2 ozs. shelled pistachio nuts

15

The day before, bone ducks and remove skin. Run duck meat, veal, pork and pork fat through a meat grinder into a large bowl. Add eggs, creme fraiche, port, rum, salt and pepper. Mix thoroughly. Pack half of mixture into a terrine or loaf pan. Slice baked ham into fingers. Place fingers lengthwise on top of mixture. Sprinkle with pistachios. Pack remaining ground mixture carefully on top of ham. Stand terrine in another pan containing hot water. Bake in 325°F. oven 2 hours. Refrigerate covered. Chill thoroughly before slicing.

To serve, slice pate 1/4-inch thick. Serve on plates with hot buttered toast. Makes 6 to 8 servings.

LES BOULETTES JACQUES
Tomato Meatballs

1 small onion, finely chopped
1 lb. ground round
1 clove garlic
4 tbs. dried bread crumbs
1 egg
salt, pepper, nutmeg
4 tbs. butter
2 small cans tomato paste
2 dry chili peppers
1/4 cup milk, about

Early in the day, place onion in a bowl with ground round. Add garlic through a press, bread crumbs and egg. Season highly with salt, pepper and nutmeg. Work the mixture well and shape into small balls. Heat butter in skillet. Fry meatballs a few at a time until they are nicely browned and well cooked, but not dry. Remove from pan. Chop chili peppers to a powder. (Do not use chili powder). To the pan in which the meatballs were cooked add tomato paste, powdered chili peppers and salt to taste. Add only enough milk to thin the sauce slightly and take up the loose fat. Return meatballs to sauce which should be thick enough to coat them heavily. Turn meatballs over and over in the sauce until they are thoroughly coated, then set aside to cool. Refrigerate if desired.

At serving time, arrange meatballs in an attractive serving dish. Stick each meatball with a toothpick and garnish with parsley. Serve cold or at room temperature, but never heated.

17

HARENG FARCI
Stuffed Pickled Herring

8 rolled pickled herrings
4 tbs. herring marinade
3 tbs. butter
4 shallots, finely chopped
1-1/2 tsp. finely chopped parsley

1/2 tsp. chopped chives
1/2 tsp. tarragon leaves
1-1/2 cups soft fresh bread crumbs
2 eggs, beaten
4 tbs. olive oil

18

Early in the day, remove herrings from jar and unroll them. Reserve 4 tablespoons of the marinade. Melt butter in a skillet. Cook shallots until tender. Add parsley, chives and tarragon. Add bread crumbs and mix well. Add eggs and mix well. Spread herrings with stuffing and re-roll them. Secure rolls with toothpicks and lay side by side, open-ends up, in a shallow baking dish. Mix together oil and the reserved marinade. Pour around fish rolls. Cover and set aside.

About 20 minutes before serving time, place herring in a 375°F. oven until fish and stuffing are heated through, about 15 to 20 minutes. Baste once or twice. Turn rolls over once. Serve hot. Makes 8 servings.

HARENG SAVOYARDE
Baked Herring and Potatoes

Early
in the
day

2 lbs. firm white potatoes
1/2 lb. Bismark herring filets
1 cup whipping cream
salt and freshly ground pepper

Early in the day, peel and shred potatoes coarsely. Drain and dry herring filets. Scrape meat from the skin and chop meat finely. Mix with potatoes and spread mixture in a lightly buttered shallow baking dish. Season cream with salt and pepper. Pour over potato mixture. Bake in 375°F. oven 50 minutes to 1 hour, or until the potatoes are thoroughly cooked and most of the cream has cooked away. Remove from oven. Cool and refrigerate.

About an hour before serving time, remove potato-herring mixture from refrigerator and bring to room temperature. Serve on small plates as the appetizer course. Makes 6 servings.

19

CRABBE MEDITERRANEE
Mediterranean Crab

1/4 lb. butter
1/4 tsp. basil
1/4 tsp. oregano
1/4 tsp. shredded green onion
1/4 tsp. chopped parsley

1/4 tsp. thyme
1/4 tsp. sage
1/2 cup dry white wine
1 lb. Alaskan crab
dry bread crumbs

An hour before serving time, melt 3 tablespoons butter in a skillet. Add basil, oregano, shredded onion, parsley, thyme, sage and wine. Cook until wine has reduced and sauce begins to dry out a little. Cut crab into bite-size chunks. Add to mixture and heat. Add 3 tablespoons butter and enough bread crumbs to hold the mixture loosely. Set aside.

About 10 minutes before serving time, place mixture in 6 baking shells or individual serving dishes. Dot with remaining 2 tablespoons butter. Place in 450°F. oven until tops are crusty and the dishes sizzling. Serve at once. Makes 6 servings.

COCKTAIL AUX FRAISES ET ANANAS
Strawberry-Pineapple Cocktail

3 ozs. strawberries
1 seedless orange
2 slices fresh pineapple
1/4 cup sugar
6 tbs. milk
1-1/2 cups dark rum
3 ozs. crushed ice

21

About an hour before serving, wash strawberries and pat dry with paper towel. Peel orange and cut into pieces. Refrigerate until needed.

Just before serving, place strawberries, orange pieces, pineapple, sugar, milk, rum and ice in blender container. Cover and blend until ice is like snow. Pour into cocktail glasses and serve immediately. Gin or vodka can be substituted for rum. Makes 6 to 8 servings.

SOUPS

Soup plays a major role in our do-it-ahead plan of meal preparation. It is versatile and need not be used merely as a meal starter, but can also serve as a hefty main dish. Soup can be served hot or cold, making it an excellent choice with which to keep warm in winter and cool on scorching summer days.

The raw materials which can be turned into soup are almost unlimited, and can run the range from a clear broth perfected from bones and vegetables to a super-sophisticated bisque prepared from lobster. There are thin soups, thick soups, soups containing virtually every product of garden and farmyard, sweet soups and sour soups.

The collection offered here is somewhat limited due to space, but I have included an unusual lettuce soup with profiteroles and a creamy chestnut soup with onion rings, as well as other delicious combinations. And best of all, their preparation is all done in advance.

It seems to me that soup has fallen into disfavor of late, and has been replaced as a meal-opener by salad. Perhaps it's time now to reverse the trend.

23

POTAGE CLERMONT
Chestnut Soup With Onion Rings

1/4 lb. butter
4 ozs. sliced celery
4 ozs. sliced onion
1-1/4 lbs. canned chestnuts or
  1 lb. 10 ozs. peeled fresh chestnuts
6 cups chicken stock
salt and pepper
1/4 lb. onions
2 cups milk
flour
6 tbs. peanut oil

The day before, melt butter in a deep saucepan over low heat. Add celery and onions. Cook until soft but not brown. Add chestnuts, stock, salt and pepper. Simmer gently 30 minutes. Pour part of soup into blender container. Cover and blend until smooth. Pour into bowl. Repeat with remaining soup until all has been blended. Refrigerate with plastic wrap pressed firmly against the surface of the soup to prevent a skin from forming. Slice onions and separate into rings. Place in a bowl and add milk. Cover and refrigerate.

About an hour before serving time, drain milk from onions into a large saucepan and set aside. Dip onion rings into flour until coated. Lay on paper toweling in a single layer. **A few minutes before serving time,** slowly warm milk over very low heat. **While milk is heating,** fry onions in hot oil. Drain on paper toweling. Add chestnut mixture to warm milk. Heat, stirring, to serving temperature. Ladle soup into bowls and garnish each serving with fried onion rings. Makes 6 servings.

One
day
ahead

POTAGE CREME DE HARICOTS VERTS
Cream of Green Bean Soup

1 lb. green beans
3 cups milk
2 tbs. butter
2 tsp. flour
grated nutmet
salt and pepper
3/4 cup chicken broth
6 tbs. creme fraiche, page 4
1 tsp. potato flour
1 egg yolk
1/2 tsp. chopped chervil

The day before, string and wash beans. Cook until tender using the Paul Mayer Method, page 5. Drain beans and reserve a few for garnish. Heat milk. Melt butter in saucepan. Add flour and cook, stirring, over low heat 2 to 3 minutes without letting flour take on any color. Remove from heat and gradually add milk, stirring constantly with a whisk. Add cooked beans. Season to taste with nutmeg, salt and pepper. Simmer gently 3 to 4 minutes. Add chicken broth. Pour part of soup into blender container. Cover and blend until smooth. Return to pan through a very fine strainer. Repeat until all soup has been blended. Heat until mixture comes to a boil. Boil 3 to 4 minutes. Combine creme fraiche and flour and add to boiling soup. Reduce heat. Beat egg yolk in a small bowl. Add a little of the hot soup. Then add egg yolk mixture to the hot, but not boiling soup, beating constantly. Cook slowly until soup thickens slightly. Finely chop reserved beans. Add to soup along with finely chopped chervil. Refrigerate with plastic wrap pressed firmly against the surface of soup to prevent a skin from forming.

At serving time, ladle into well-chilled bowls or gently reheat, but do not boil, until hot. Serve immediately. Makes 6 servings.

One
day
ahead

POTAGE TOURANGELLE
Green Bean Soup with Shredded Lettuce

3/4 lb. dry white beans
2 lbs. green beans
1/4 cup butter
2 tsp. flour
3/4 cup bean liquid
pepper
6 tbs. creme fraiche, page 4
1 egg yolk
juice of 1/2 lemon
1 tbs. chopped parsley
2-1/2 cups milk

Before starting soup, soak dry beans overnight or for several hours in cold water. Drain and cover with fresh, salted water. Bring to a boil. Cook slowly 1-1/2 hours. Drain thoroughly and set aside. String green beans and cut into pieces. Cook according to the Paul Mayer Method, page 5. Drain beans and reserve 3/4 cup cooking liquid. Melt butter in saucepan. Stir in flour and cook slowly 3 or 4 minutes without letting the flour color. Remove from heat and stir in reserved liquid a little at a time. Return to heat and simmer 10 minutes. Season with pepper. Combine creme fraiche and egg yolk. Add a little of the hot sauce to the mixture. Stir back into sauce. Cook, stirring, until mixture thickens. Add lemon juice. Combine beans, green beans, sauce and milk. Stir well. Pour part of mixture into blender container. Cover and blend until smooth. Pour into bowl. Repeat until all of the soup has been blended. Refrigerate with plastic wrap pressed firmly against the surface of soup.

Serve cold with Shredded Lettuce Garnish, or reheat slowly without boiling. Garnish hot soup with croutons. Makes 6 servings.

Shredded Lettuce Garnish

Shred 1 small head of lettuce. Place in a pot with chicken broth to cover. Bring slowly to boil. Immediately drain and rinse quickly with cold water. Drain thoroughly. Add to cold soup just before serving.

CREME D'ARTICHAUT FROIDE
Chilled Cream of Artichoke Soup

6 artichokes
1 tomato
1/4 lb. butter
2 onions, sliced
3 leeks, sliced

1 tsp. curry powder
1/4 lb. raw rice
12 cups bouillon
2 cups milk

30

The day before, break leaves from uncooked artichokes. Remove core and the choke. Trim and slice the artichoke bottoms. Peel, seed and slice tomato. Melt butter in a large saucepan. Add onion, leeks, tomato and artichoke slices. Stew in butter 15 minutes. Add curry powder, rice, bouillon and milk. Boil 40 minutes. Pour part of mixture into blender container. Cover and blend until smooth. Pour into bowl. Repeat with remaining soup until all has been blended. Refrigerate with plastic wrap pressed firmly against the surface of soup to prevent a skin from forming.

To serve, ladle cold soup into well chilled bowls. Serve immediately. Makes 8 to 12 servings.

One
day
ahead

CREME BREALOISE
Cream of Lettuce Soup

2 heads (10 ozs. ea.) lettuce, sliced
2 tsp. dry chervil
2-1/4 lbs. shelled peas (fresh or frozen)
4 cups chicken broth
6 egg yolks
2 cups creme fraiche, page 4
Profiteroles, page 33

The day before, cook lettuce, chervil and peas in boiling salted water 25 minutes. Drain off water and replace it with chicken broth. Cook 10 minutes. Pour part of mixture into blender container. Cover and blend until smooth. Repeat with remaining mixture. Pour soup into pan through an extremely fine sieve to eliminate pea skins. Beat egg yolks and creme fraiche together. Add to soup and cook, stirring, until mixture thickens. Do not let it boil. Pour into large bowl and cover with plastic wrap pressed firmly against surface of soup. Refrigerate.

Just before serving time, slowly reheat soup, stirring occasionally. Do not boil. Serve soup hot with Profiteroles floating on each serving. Makes 8 servings.

Profiteroles

1/2 cup water
1/4 cup butter
salt and pepper
1/2 cup flour (scant)

In the afternoon, heat water, butter, salt and pepper together in saucepan. When boiling, add flour all at once. Remove from heat and beat steadily until mixture forms a smooth, shiny ball and leaves the sides of the pan. Add eggs one at a time, beating well after adding the last egg. Grease a cookie sheet. Using a pastry bag with a small plain tube, pipe out 24 small balls of dough onto cookie sheet. Bake in 425°F. oven 10 minutes. Turn off heat and leave in oven at least 25 minutes longer. Remove from oven and store uncovered, until needed. Serve floating on Creme Brealoise. Makes 24.

VELOUTE DE CHAMPIGNONS
Cream of Mushroom Soup

1/2 lb. mushrooms
juice of 1 lemon
2 large onions, chopped
2 tbs. butter
2 tbs. flour
4 cups chicken broth
2 cups water
2 egg yolks
6 tbs. creme fraiche, page 4

The day before, chop mushrooms and moisten them with lemon juice. Melt butter in a large saucepan. Slowly cook onion and mushrooms in butter without letting them brown. Cook until very soft. Add flour and cook gently 2 minutes. Stir in chicken broth and water. Season with salt and pepper. Boil fairly rapidly 20 minutes. Pour part of soup into blender container. Cover and blend until smooth. Return mixture to pan through a fine strainer to remove small particles. Repeat process until all soup has been blended. Beat egg yolks and creme fraiche together. Add a little hot soup, then stir briskly back into soup. Cook over low heat, stirring occasionally, until thickened. Pour into a bowl and cover with plastic wrap pressed firmly against surface. Refrigerate.

Just before serving time, slowly reheat soup stirring occasionally. Do not let mixture boil. Serve hot. Makes 6 servings.

POTAGE BLESOISE
Pea Soup with Barley, Mushrooms and Carrots

1 qt. chicken broth
1/4 lb. barley
1/4 lb. large mushrooms
1/4 lb. carrots

1 pkg. (16 ozs.) tiny frozen peas
6 tbs. creme fraiche, page 4
salt and pepper

The day before, combine broth and barley in large saucepan. Bring to boil. Cover and cook slowly 45 minutes. Cut mushrooms and carrots into julienne. Cook separately in boiling, salted water about 5 minutes or until tender. Drain thoroughly and set aside. Cook peas in boiling, salted water 5 minutes. Drain and add to cooked barley and its broth. Pour into blender container. Cover and blend until smooth. If mixture is too thick add enough extra broth (up to 4 cups if necessary) to thin to a good soup consistency. Add creme fraiche. Season to taste with salt and pepper. Strain soup through an extremely fine sieve to remove pea skins and barley bits. Add carrots and mushrooms to soup. Refrigerate with plastic wrap pressed firmly against the surface of soup.

Just before serving time, slowly reheat soup. Do not boil. Makes 8 to 12 servings.

POTAGE MADELON
Split Pea and Tomato Soup

One day ahead

14 ozs. split peas
1/4 lb. onions, sliced
2 leeks sliced
2 ozs. sliced carrots
7 tbs. butter

1 lb. tomatoes
2 qts. beef stock
1 qt. water
salt and pepper
2 ozs. tapioca

Before starting soup, soak peas overnight or for several hours in cold water. Drain before using. Melt butter in deep pot. Add onions, leeks and carrots. Braise 10 minutes over low heat without letting them brown. Peel, seed and chop tomatoes. Add drained peas and tomatoes to braised vegetables. Stir in stock and water. Season to taste with salt and pepper. Cook briskly 50 minutes, uncovered. Pour part of soup into blender container. Cover and blend until smooth. Repeat until all soup has been blended. Return soup to pot and add tapioca. Boil 10 minutes. Refrigerate with plastic wrap pressed firmly against surface of soup to prevent a skin from forming.

Just before serving time, reheat soup slowly, stirring occasionally. Serve immediately.

A GRAND APPROCH
TO A CHATEAU
CHENONCEAUX

EGGS

There is a restaurant in the Parisian suburb, Pontchartrain, whose proprietor keeps hens who lay eggs on command. This remarkable feat is performed daily as part of a show for the amusement of his guests, and I imagine that there are no fresher eggs in the world.

But whether minutes or several days old, eggs play an even larger role in the French pattern of dining than perhaps anywhere else on the globe. The American cook tends to relegate eggs to the breakfast table, with an occasional foray onto the brunch or luncheon scene, but with today's high prices of meat there is more and more reason for investigating the many dishes which can be prepared from boiled, fried, baked or scrambled eggs.

Eggs can find a place not only at the morning table, but as a first course, main dish and in numerous desserts such as glorious souffles, Baked Alaska and even that bane of most childhoods, Floating Island.

OEUFS POCHES EN MEURETTE
Poached Eggs in Red Wine Sauce

1 fifth Beaujolais <u>or</u> light Burgundy
12 eggs
parsley, thyme, bay leaf
1 tbs. butter
1-1/2 tbs. flour
2 ozs. shallots, chopped
1 tsp. meat glaze or bovril
1 tsp. tomato paste
salt and pepper
12 slices day-old bread
6 tbs. butter, melted
1 clove garlic, cut in half
2 tsp. chopped parsley

40

An hour or two before serving time, bring wine to boil in an enameled or tin-lined copper skillet. (Do not use cast iron or aluminum.) Place eggs, still in their shells, in boiling wine for 10 seconds. Remove eggs and reduce heat. Break eggs one-by-one into barely boiling wine. Poach 3 minutes. Lift poached eggs from wine and keep in a bowl of tap water. Eggs may be kept in this manner for several hours. Rewarm by placing in hot tap water for a few minutes. Change the water as it cools. Tie parsley, thyme and bay leaf in cheese cloth and add to wine. Increase temperature and reduce wine by one half. Knead butter and flour together. Stir into reduced wine along with shallots, meat glaze, tomato paste, salt and pepper. Simmer until sauce reaches a pleasing consistency. Strain through an extremely fine sieve. Set aside covered with plastic wrap pressed firmly against surface to prevent skin from forming.

Just before serving time, slowly reheat sauce. Cut rounds the size of the eggs from bread slices. Melt butter in skillet. Add bread slices and turn them over immediately so both sides are coated with butter. Then increase heat and brown on both sides. Rub lightly with cut garlic. Arrange toast rounds on serving dish. Place a warm poached egg on each round and generously coat with reheated sauce. Sprinkle with parsley Makes 6 servings.

LES OEUFS POCHES TOURANGELLE
Mushroom Caps with Poached Eggs and Mornay Sauce

Mornay Sauce, page 43
6 eggs, poached (see page 40)
6 giant mushrooms
1/4 lb. butter

Early in the day, prepare Sauce Mornay as directed. Pour into a bowl and cover with plastic wrap pressed tightly against surface to prevent a skin from forming. Refrigerate until needed. **About half an hour before serving time,** reheat sauce in double boiler over hot water. Poach eggs and keep warm in a bowl of hot tap water. Replace water as it cools. Rinse mushrooms. Dry with paper toweling and remove stems.

Just before serving time, melt butter in frying pan and saute mushrooms 15 minutes. Turn frequently as they cook. Arrange sauteed mushrooms on a flameproof serving dish. Drain and dry eggs. Place an egg on each mushroom. Coat with Sauce Mornay. Place under broiler to quickly brown. Serve at once. Makes 6 servings.

Mornay Sauce

1/4 cup butter
1/4 cup flour
2 cups milk
1 cup (1/2 pt.) whipping cream
salt and pepper
3 egg yolks
2 ozs. imported Parmesan, grated

Melt butter in saucepan over medium heat. Blend in flour. Remove from heat and gradually stir in milk, whipping cream, salt and pepper. Bring to a boil, stirring constantly. Reduce heat and simmer 30 minutes, stirring occasionally. Beat egg yolks in small bowl. Add a little of the hot sauce to yolks. Slowly pour mixture back into hot sauce, beating as you pour. Do not let sauce boil. Add Parmesan and stir until it melts. Use sauce as directed.

OEUFS POCHES ARCHIDUC
Tarts with Poached Eggs and Chicken Livers

6 tartlets, page 45
6 eggs, poached (see page 40)
1 tsp. white vinegar
6 raw chicken livers
8 tbs. butter
1 tbs. brandy
1 onion, finely chopped
6 tbs. creme fraiche, page 4
1/4 tsp. potato flour
1 tsp. paprika
parsley springs

44

Early in the day, prepare Pate a Foncer and make into tartlets as directed. **About an hour before serving,** poach eggs and keep warm in hot tap water. Slice livers. Melt butter in skillet over high heat. When very hot, add livers a few at a time and brown quickly. Remove from pan as they brown. When all are brown return to pan. Pour brandy over livers and ignite. Remove livers. Cover and keep warm. Drain pan and add remaining butter.

Saute onions 5 minutes. Add creme fraiche, potato flour and paprika. Cook 5 minutes. Strain into bowl and cover with plastic wrap pressed firmly against the surface to prevent a skin from forming. Keep warn over hot water.

When ready to serve, drain and dry eggs. Place livers in tartlets. Top with poached eggs. Spoon sauce over eggs to cover. Serve immediately. Makes 6 servings.

Pate a Foncer—Basic Pastry

1 cup flour
10 tbs. butter
salt
3 tbs. cold water

Measure flour into bowl. Using a pastry blender, work butter carefully into flour. Add a little salt and gather dough gently by sprinkling it with cold water. Let rest for 1 hour. Roll dough out into a circle. Cut to fit 6 medium-sized tartlet pans. Bake tartlets in 350°F. oven 10 minutes. Remove from oven. Cool and cover loosely until needed.

M. NELSON

OEUFS DUR A LA COMMERE
Hard-Cooked Eggs with Potatoes and Onion Sauce

1/2 lb. onions
14 tbs. butter
1/2 lb. potatoes
12 tbs. creme fraiche, page 4

salt and pepper
12 hard-cooked eggs
4 ozs. imported Parmesan, grated

About an hour before serving time, thinly slice onions. Melt 6 tablespoons butter in a skillet with cover, over low heat. Add onions. Cover and gently stew 30 minutes. Peel and quarter potatoes. Cook in boiling, salted water 20 minutes. Drain and put through a food mill or fine sieve. Add 6 tablespoons <u>each</u> butter and creme fraiche. Season to taste and set aside. When onions are cooked, add remaining creme fraiche and season to taste. Put into blender container. Cover and puree. Peel eggs and cut in half. Coat a baking dish with remaining 2 tablespoons butter. Spread potato puree over bottom of dish. Arrange eggs, cut side down, on potato puree. Cover eggs with onion sauce. Sprinkle with Parmesan. Cover with plastic wrap and set aside.

Ten minutes before serving time, bake in 375°F. oven 10 minutes or until thoroughly heated. Serve immediately. Makes 6 servings.

47

OEUFS BROUILLES BALZAC
Scrambled Eggs with Tongue and Truffles

12 eggs
1 small can truffles, undrained
2 medium tomatoes, peeled
6 slices day-old bread
11 tbs. butter
1 oz. imported Parmesan, grated
4 ozs. cooked tongue, julienned

Two or three hours before serving, beat eggs in a large bowl. Drain truffle juice into bowl with eggs. Cut truffles into julienne and add to eggs. Cover and refrigerate. **Shortly before serving time,** cut tomatoes into 3 slices each. Cut bread into rounds the same size as tomatoes. Melt 4 tablespoons butter in skillet. Add bread rounds and turn immediately so both sides are coated with butter. Increase heat and brown on both sides. Place in shallow baking pan and set aside.

Just before serving time, arrange tomato slices on top of bread rounds. Sprinkle with cheese and drizzle any butter left in skillet over the top. Melt 7 tablespoons butter in the top of double broiler over hot water. Add egg-truffle mixture and beat with a whisk until softly scrambled. Add tongue. Broil tomato garnishes until cheese is toasted. Arrange scrambled eggs on a warm platter. Make a crown of the tomato-toast garnishes on top of eggs. Serve immediately. Makes 6 servings.

OMELETTE LORRAINE
Bacon, Cheese and Chive Omelet

1/4 lb. bacon
6 ozs. Gruyere cheese
12 eggs
12 tbs. melted butter

Early in the day, cut bacon into small fingers and cook until crisp. Drain on absorbent paper. Cut half of Gruyere into tiny slices and grate the remainder. Cover bacon and cheese and set aside. Beat eggs in large bowl and refrigerate, covered.

Just before serving time, add bacon, cheese and chives to eggs. Using omelet pan, make 6 individual omelets. Arrange finished omelets on flameproof serving dishes. Sprinkle 1-1/2 tablespoons grated cheese and 2 tablespoons melted butter over each omelet. Place under hot broiler to melt cheese and lightly brown omelets. Serve immediately.

OMELETTE AUX CREVETTES
Shrimp Omelet

8 tbs. butter
1/4 lb. tiny shrimp
1/4 lb. mushrooms, julienned
12 eggs

An hour before serving time, melt 2 tablespoons butter in skillet. When foaming, add shrimp and cook 5 minutes. Remove from pan and set aside. Increase heat and add 2 tablespoons butter to skillet. When very hot, add mushrooms and cook 5 minutes. Remove from heat. Combine shrimp with mushrooms and set aside.

At serving time, warm shrimp and mushrooms over low heat. Break eggs into large bowl and beat until blended. Stir shrimp and mushrooms into eggs. Using omelet pan make one huge, or 4 or 6 individual omelets. Brown remaining butter over high heat. Pour over omelets and serve immediately. Makes 4 to 6 servings.

51

OEUFS COCOTTE CHANTILLY
Baked Eggs with Peas and Hollandaise

1 pkg. (10 ozs.) frozen peas
2 tbs. creme fraiche, page 4
12 eggs
3 egg yolks
6 tbs. soft butter
salt and cayenne pepper

Early in the day, cook peas in boiling, salted water 15 minutes. Drain well. Put through a food mill and then puree in blender. Pour into mixing bowl. Season pureed peas with salt and pepper. Stir in creme fraiche and refrigerate, covered with plastic wrap pressed firmly against the surface of mixture to prevent a skin from forming. **About an hour before serving time,** butter 12 individual ramekins. Place a spoonful of puree in the bottom of each ramekin. Press a small piece of plastic wrap tightly against mixture. Let stand at room temperature until needed.

About twenty minutes before serving time, set ramekins in a large pan containing boiling water. Place in 350°F. oven 10 minutes. Break an egg into each ramekin and return

to oven for an additional 10 minutes. **While eggs are baking,** combine egg yolks, butter, salt and cayenne in a small, heavy saucepan. Stir over lowest heat until sauce thickens. Do not boil. Spoon enough sauce over each egg to cover. Place ramekins under broiler until sauce browns. Serve hot and at once. Makes 6 servings.

FISHING
OUT OF
LE PALAIS ON
BELLE ILE
M. NELSON 76

FISH

Fish does not lend itself as readily to advance preparation as do most other foods. Delicate by nature, both fish and shellfish tend to lose flavor and texture if cooked in advance and allowed to rest for too long. However, in some cases this may be accomplished with excellent results, and in others, the actural cooking time involved is minimal once the advance preparation has taken place.

Also, there are many seafood dishes which may be served cold and these, of course, may be finished ahead of time.

The oceans and streams of the world yield many varieties of fish and so we have included here, once again, dishes which can be served hot or cold, poached, baked, sauteed and fried. We run the gamut from oysters to salmon and tuna, from prawns to sole, and in each case you will find that contrary to being time consuming at the dinner hour, these dishes will take relatively little final preparation.

TRUITE FARCI MATIGNON
Cheese-Stuffed Trout with Fried Tomatoes

Mornay Sauce, page 43
6 whole trout, boned
salt and pepper
3 small tomatoes
8 tbs. butter
7 tbs. oil
2 ozs. almonds, finely chopped
2 eggs
1 tsp. water
flour
dry bread-crumbs
lemon slices

56

The day before, prepare Mornay Sauce and refrigerate with plastic wrap pressed firmly against the surface to prevent a skin from forming. **Early in the day,** spread trout flat with heads, skin and tails still intact. Season with salt and pepper. Fill each trout with as much

Mornay Sauce as it will hold. Refrigerate covered. **An hour before serving time,** peel and slice each tomato into 6 slices. Remove seeds. Combine eggs and water. Dredge tomato slices in flour, dip in beaten egg, then coat with crumbs. Set aside.

   Just before serving time, melt 2 tablespoons butter in large skillet over medium heat. Add 1 tablespoon oil. Saute tomato slices, a few at a time, until lightly browned on each side. Add more butter and oil if needed. **While tomatoes are cooking,** melt 6 tablespoons butter in large skillet over medium heat. Cook trout until nicely browned on both sides. Arrange trout on a large, warm platter. Lay cooked tomato slices, overlapping, on top of trout. Set into warm oven. Add almonds to skillet and quickly cook in pan drippings until golden. Spoon over fish. Garnish with lemon slices. Makes 6 servings.

FILET DE SOLE CUSSUY
Wine-Poached Sole with Vegetable Sauce

2 ozs. carrots
2 ozs. leeks (white only)
1 oz. celery
4 ozs. mushrooms
4 tbs. butter
12 tbs. fish stock, page 59

2 ozs. shallots, chopped
12 small sole fillets
3/4 cup Riesling wine
2 tsp. potato flour
3/4 cup creme fraiche, page 4

Early in the afternoon, peel carrots and remove cores. Cut carrots, leeks, celery and mushrooms into fine julienne. Melt butter in small Dutch oven. Add vegetables and 6 tablespoons fish stock. Cook uncovered over gentle heat 20 minutes. Remove from heat. Drain vegetables and set aside. Reserve liquid.

One half hour before serving time, butter an ovenproof baking dish. Sprinkle the bottom with shallots. Lay sole fillets on top of shallots. Pour Riesling and the remaining 6 tablespoons stock over fish. Sprinkle with salt and pepper. Cover closely with waxed paper and bake in 325°F. oven 15 minutes. Remove from oven. Drain off liquid and reserve. Arrange poached fish on a heatproof serving platter. Return to oven, with the heat off, to keep warm. Combine fish liquid with reserved vegetable liquid. Boil over high heat until reduced by half. Combine potato flour and creme fraiche and add to reduced liquid. Bring to boil, stirring constantly, until sauce thickens. Strain and combine with vegetables. Heat gently. Spread sauce over fish and serve immediately. Makes 6 servings.

FISH STOCK

2 lbs. fish heads and trimmings
8 cups water
2 onions, chopped
2 carrots, chopped
3 stalks celery, chopped
3 or 4 peppercorns
salt

   Place ingredients in large kettle over medium heat. Bring to boil. Reduce heat and cook, uncovered, until stock has reduced to 4 cups. Strain and use or freeze in 1 cup portions for future use. Makes 4 cups.

FILET DE SOLE RICHARDIN
Sole with Mushrooms, Caper-Gherkin Garnish

7 ozs. mushrooms
2 ozs. gherkins
1 oz. capers
12 small sole fillets
salt, pepper, paprika

flour
8 tbs. butter
2 ozs. sliced almonds
1 tbs. chopped parsley

60

Early in the day, slice mushrooms and dice gherkins. Wrap in plastic and set aside. Measure capers into small dish and set aside.

About half an hour before serving time, season sole with salt, pepper and paprika. Dredge lightly in flour. Spank fillets to remove excess flour. Melt 4 tablespoons butter in skillet. Gently cook fish five minutes on each side. Arrange on serving platter. Place in low oven to keep warm. Add mushrooms to skillet and cook over high heat 10 minutes. While mushrooms are cooking melt remaining butter in small skillet. Add almonds and cook until golden brown. Spoon mushrooms over fish. Sprinkle with gherkins and capers. Pour almonds and butter over all. Sprinkle with chopped parsley. Serve immediately while hot. Makes 6 servings.

CREVETTES LUCIFER
Fried Shrimp with Minted Hollandaise

1-1/4 lbs. medium shrimp
flour
3 eggs, beaten
dried bread crumbs
4 egg yolks
1 tbs. wine vinegar

1 tsp. finely chopped mint
1 tbs. water
2 tbs. creme fraiche, page 4
7 tbs. soft butter
salt, cayenne pepper
deep hot fat

61

In the afternoon, shell and devein shrimp. Dredge in flour. Spank off excess. Dip in beaten eggs, then roll in crumbs. Shake to remove excess crumbs. Refrigerate. **About an hour before serving time,** make Sauce Paloise by combining egg yolks, vinegar, mint, water, creme fraiche, butter, salt and cayenne in the top of a double boiler. Cook over boiling water, beating briskly with a wire whisk until sauce thickens to a nice consistency. Keep warm over hot, not boiling, water.

About twenty minutes before serving time, heat fat to 350°F. Fry shrimp, a few at a time, for 5 minutes. Drain on absorbent paper. Lay a large, folded cloth napkin on a serving plate as you would for keeping rolls hot. Lay shrimp on napkin. Fold end over to cover and keep warm. Serve sauce separately. Makes 6 servings.

MEDAILLON DE SAUMON GENEVOISE
Medallion of Salmon Genoa-Style

7 tbs. butter
2-1/4 lbs. fish heads
5 ozs. thinkly sliced carrots
2 ozs. sliced shallots
7 ozs. sliced onion
4 ozs. sliced mushrooms
2 fifths red Burgundy
4 cups fish stock, page 59
4 tsp. tomato paste
salt and pepper

1 (1-1/4 lbs.) live lobster
2-1/2 tbs. flour
6 tbs. creme fraiche, page 4
1/2 tsp. potato starch
8 tbs. butter
4 tsp. sugar
30 tiny button mushrooms
30 tiny onions
6 (4 ozs. ea.) salmon fillets
finely chopped parsley

In the early afternoon, melt 7 tablespoons butter in Dutch oven. Add fish heads, carrots, shallots, onions and mushrooms. Stir in Burgundy, <u>2</u> cups fish stock, tomato paste, salt and pepper. Bring to boil and drop in lobster. Cover and cook 25 minutes. Remove lobster and set aside. **During the time the lobster is cooking,** melt 4 tablespoons butter in saucepan. Add flour and cook gently 5 minutes. Blend in remaining 2 cups fish stock. Stir until sauce boils. Lower heat and cook gently 30 minutes. Add creme fraiche and potato starch. Cook 10 minutes. Strain into lobster liquid and cook uncovered 45 minutes. Remove lobster meat from shell and add shell to sauce. Cook 15 minutes. Cut lobster meat into pieces and refrigerate. Strain sauce and refrigerate. **About an hour before serving time,** melt 2 tablespoons butter in skillet over high heat. Cook mushrooms 15 minutes or until moisture has cooked away and mushrooms are browned. Set aside. In another skillet melt 2 tablespoons butter. Add sugar, onions and 2 cups water. Boil, uncovered, until water has cooked away. Set aside.

Half an hour before serving time, melt remaining butter in a skillet over low heat. Gently cook salmon fillets 10 minutes on each side without allowing to brown. Reheat sauce. Arrange salmon on an ovenproof serving dish. Top each fillet with 5 mushrooms, 5 tiny onions and pieces of lobster meat. Pour warmed sauce over all. Place in 300ºF. oven 10 minutes or until thoroughly heated. Sprinkle with finely chopped parsley. Serve immediately. Makes 6 servings.

FILET DE FLETAN FANCHON
Halibut on Spinach with Pickle-Chive Garnish

1-1/4 lbs. fresh spinach
6 halibut or salmon steaks or fillets
flour
3 eggs beaten with 1 tsp. water

bread crumbs
1/2 lb. butter
2 ozs. gherkins, julienned
2 tsp. chopped chives

Early in the day, wash spinach thoroughly. Cook in boiling salted water 10 minutes. Pour into colander to drain and cool. When cool enough to handle, squeeze spinach until completely moisture-free. Cover with plastic wrap and set aside. **About an hour before serving,** dredge halibut lightly in flour, then in beaten eggs. Finally roll in bread crumbs until nicely coated on all sides. Spank to remove excess crumbs. Cover loosely and set aside at room temperature.

Just before serving time, melt 6 tablespoons butter in a small skillet. Toss spinach with butter and cook 5 minutes. Melt 7 tablespoons butter in a large skillet until foaming. Cook fish 5 minutes on each side. Transfer spinach to a round serving dish. Arrange fish on top of spinach. Sprinkle with gherkins and chives. Pour remaining, lightly browned butter over the top and serve immediately. Makes 6 servings.

TOURNEDOS DE PECHEUR
Tuna Steaks with Garlic-Potato Sauce

6 pieces (6 ozs. ea.) fresh tuna
6 slices bacon
garlic
anchovies
peanut oil
bay leaf

sprigs of thyme
coarsely chopped parsley
whole peppercorns
chopped chives
Sauce Rouille, page 67
6 tbs. butter

The day before, remove skin from fish. Tie fish into rounds, placing a piece of bacon around them in the same manner as a filet mignon is wrapped. Make 6 slits in each fillet and insert 3 slivers of garlic and 3 small pieces of anchovy. Place fish rounds, single layer, in a shallow dish. Pour enough oil over them to come about one quarter way up the thickeness of the fish. Cover each piece heavily with bay leaf, thyme, parsley and peppercorns. Cover with plastic wrap and refrigerate. Turn once or twice while marinating. **The next afternoon,** prepare Sauce Rouille as directed. Cover and hold at room temperature until serving time.

About half an hour before serving time, melt butter in skillet. When it is foaming, cook fish tournedos 15 minutes. turning frequently. Serve with freshly boiled potatoes and Sauce Rouille. Makes 6 servings.

Sauce Rouille

2 boiled potatoes
2 cloves garlic
salt and cayenne
2 egg yolks
1 cup oil

Put potatoes through a ricer or Foley food mill into large electric mixer bowl. Add garlic through a press, salt and cayenne. Beat until smooth. Add egg yolks. Beat well. Add oil, a little at a time, beating constantly as for mayonnaise. Cover and hold at room temperature.

HOMARD PAIMPOLAISE
Lobster in Cream Hollandaise

3 (1-1/4 lbs. ea.) live Maine lobsters *
5 tbs. butter
1/2 lb. tomatoes
1/2 cup Cognac
2 tsp. chopped parsley
2 tsp. chopped chives
1/2 cup Madeira
3/4 cup chicken broth

2 cups cream fraiche, page 4
1 to 2 tbs. potato flour
4 egg yolks
1/2 lb. butter
1 tsp. lemon juice
1/4 cup cream
salt and cayenne pepper

68

Early in the day, or as soon as you bring lobster home, melt 5 tablespoons butter in Dutch oven. Add lobster pieces, shell and all. Cover and cook, turning frequently, until lobster turns bright red. Remove from heat. Peel, seed and chop tomatoes. Add to lobster and return to heat. Pour in Cognac and warm it. Ignite and when flame goes out, add parsley, chives, Madeira, chicken broth, salt and pepper. Cover and cook 15 minutes. Add creme fraiche. Cook 15 minutes longer. Lift lobster pieces from sauce and set aside to cool. Bring sauce to a boil. Mix potato flour with a little water. Add to boiling sauce. Cook, stirring, until mixture reaches a nice consistency. Remove from heat. Cover with plastic wrap pressed firmly against surface of sauce and refrigerate. When lobster has cooled enough to handle, remove meat from shells. Refrigerate. Prepare a hollandaise by placing egg yolks, butter, lemon juice, cream, salt and cayenne in a deep, heavy saucepan. Stir over gentle heat until mixture thickens and has a custard-like consistency. Combine hollandiase and cream sauce. Add lobster and mix thoroughly. Cover with plastic wrap pressed firmly against surface and refrigerate.

Just before serving time, carefully reheat lobster sauce over hot water. Serve in the center of a rice ring. Makes 6 servings.

* Live Maine lobsters usually have to be ordered in advance. Have them killed while you wait and cut up as follows. The tail in 3 pieces, claws in 3 pieces at the joints, and the remaining piece in half lengthwise. Discard sac and eyes. Cook immediately as uncooked lobster does not keep well.

BEIGNETS D'HUITRES LA VARENNE
Fried Stuffed Oysters

72 fresh oysters, shelled
4 tbs. butter
1 oz. shallots, chopped
1/2 lb. mushrooms, chopped
6 tbs. Chablis
salt and pepper
2 egg yolks

1 oz. stale bread
1 cup sifted flour
6 tbs. beer
2 eggs, separated
Sauce Bearnaise, page 71
deep hot fat

70

Early in the day, place oysters in a small pan with their liquor. Poach until edges begin to curl. Drain and dry on absorbent paper. Cover and refrigerate. Melt butter in small Dutch oven. Add shallots, mushrooms and Chablis. Season with salt and pepper. Cook 10 minutes or until liquid has evaporated. Add egg yolks and stale bread, which has been soaked in warm water and squeezed dry. Mix well. Spread mixture on a plate. Cover with plastic wrap pressed against the surface. Refrigerate until chilled. Make 36 "oyster sandwiches" by placing some of the mixture between 2 oysters and pressing them gently together. Cover and refrigerate. **About an hour and a half before cooking time,** combine flour, beer, egg yolks, salt and pepper in mixing bowl. Beat until smooth. Let rest 1 hour. Prepare Sauce

Bearnaise as directed. Keep warm over hot, not boiling water.

About fifteen minutes before serving time, heat fat to 350°F. Beat egg whites until stiff. Fold into batter. Dip "oyster sandwiches" into fritter batter. Fry in hot fat 2 minutes. Drain on absorbent paper and keep warm. Arrange on serving platter. Serve with Bearnaise Sauce. Makes 6 to 8 servings.

Bearnaise Sauce

3 shallots, chopped	1 tsp. <u>each</u> parsley,
1/2 cup vinegar	chives and tarragon
2 egg yolks	salt and cayenne
2 tbs. cream	8 tbs. butter

Combine shallots and vinegar in small saucepan. Boil until vinegar measures 2 tablespoons. Strain into small, heavy pan. Add remaining ingredients. Stir over low heat until mixture thickens. Do not boil.

SIGHTSEEING
FRANCE
M. NELSON 76

POULTRY

The chicken is a gregarious fellow! He gets along well with his culinary neighbors. Young, middle-aged or old the chicken can be transformed into a taste-tempting, eye-pleasing dish when served alone or with seafood, vegetables, pastry or spaghetti. Nearly everyone likes chicken, and as a result, the search for new recipes for this popular dish is always with us.

To be sure, there are other fowl which grace dinner tables throughout the world, and in presenting some new and intersting methods of serving poultry, we have tried not to neglect them. Although, for example, the turkey seems to be almost exclusively American, you will find here a French recipe which will surely be welcome on any Thanksgiving Day table. And, duck, properly prepared, can transend even chicken as a festive offering.

Most of the work involved in poultry preparation is preliminary, and the birds need little attention during cooking. This eminently qualifies chicken, duck and turkey for a place in a book devoted to getting things done before company rings the doorbell.

FRICASSEE DE POULET
Chicken Fricassee

7 tbs. butter
4 lb. chicken, cut up
12 small white onions
2 tbs. Armagnac or other brandy
6 tbs. white wine

6 tbs. concentrated chicken stock
5 ozs. pitted green olives
1/2 lb. small mushroom caps
1 tsp. potato flour
3 tbs. water

74

Early in the day, melt butter in a Dutch oven. Add chicken pieces and onions. Brown thoroughly. Pour Armagnac over chicken and ignite. When flame dies add wine, chicken stock, olives and mushrooms. Cover and refrigerate.

An hour before serving time, place the pot of chicken, covered, in oven. Turn heat to 350°F and cook 45 minutes. Remove from oven and place chicken pieces on serving plate. Cover with foil and return to oven with heat off, to keep warm. Place Dutch oven over direct heat and bring sauce to boil. Dissolve potato flour in water. Add to boiling sauce. Cook, stirring, until sauce thickens. Arrange mushrooms and olives over chicken. Spoon sauce over all and serve immediately. Makes 6 servings.

POULET BASQUAISE
Chicken In Wine With Peppers, Onions and Tomatoes

4 tbs. peanut oil
4 lb. chicken, cup up
3/4 cup dry white wine
salt, pepper, sugar
1/2 tsp. thyme

1 bay leaf
4 sprigs parsley
1 lb. green or red peppers
1 lb. each onions and tomatoes
1 clove garlic

In the afternoon, heat 2 tablespoons oil in a Dutch oven. Brown chicken pieces. Add wine. Season with salt and pepper. Tie thyme, bay leaf and parsley in a small piece of cheesecloth. Add to chicken. Cover pot and bake in 325°F. oven 25 minutes. **While chicken is in the oven,** cut peppers in large julienne. Slice onions, and peel, seed and chop tomatoes. Heat remaining oil in large skillet. Add vegetables and garlic through a press. Season with salt, pepper and a pinch of sugar. Cook briskly until all moisture has evaporated. Remove chicken from oven. Add vegetables to chicken and set aside.

Forty-five minutes before serving time, return chicken and vegetables to 325°F. oven. Cook, covered 40 minutes. Arrange chicken on serving dish. Cover with vegetables. Garnish with parsley. Makes 6 servings.

75

POULARDE FARCI AUX TRUFFES
Roast Chicken with Pork, Veal-Truffle Stuffing

4 ozs. <u>each</u> pork filet and veal
1 small can truffles
3 tbs. milk
2 Royal Lunch crackers
1 egg

1-1/2 tbs. Cognac
salt and pepper
4 lb. chicken
3 tbs. butter
6 tbs. chicken stock

76

Early in the day, grind pork, veal and truffles. Mix together well. Heat milk and add crackers. Allow to soak until doubled in size. Squeeze dry. Mix squeezed crackers, egg, Cognac, salt, pepper and meat. Refrigerate. **About 2 hours before serving time,** salt inside of chicken. Stuff with filling and close opening. Melt butter in flat baking dish, place chicken in dish and roast in 325°F. oven 90 minutes. Baste frequently. Remove chicken from oven. Cut opening so stuffing can be removed intact.

To serve, cut stuffing in 6 slices. Place chicken on large platter. Arrange stuffing slices leaning against the chicken on both sides. Heat stock in roasting pan to deglaze it. Season. Strain juices and serve separately. Makes 6 servings.

POULET SAUTE CYNTHIA
Chicken in Champagne with Grapes and Oranges

In the after-noon

9 tbs. butter
3-1/2 lb. chicken, cut up
1 tsp. potato flour
3/4 cup dry champagne
1 chicken bouillon cube

juice of 1/2 lemon
1 tbs. Curacao
salt and pepper
24 seedless grapes
24 Mandarin orange sections

About 2 hours before serving time, melt 5 tablespoons butter in Dutch oven. Add chicken pieces and coat well with butter. Place uncovered in 325°F. oven 50 minutes. Turn pieces occasionally. When chicken is nicely browned and tender, remove from pot. Place pot over direct heat. Blend in potato flour. Add champagne, bouillon cube, lemon juice and Curacao. Season to taste with salt and pepper. Cook, stirring, until sauce comes to a boil and thickens. Add grapes and oranges and remaining 4 tablespoons butter. Return chicken to sauce and keep warm over hot water, but no longer than 1 hour.

At serving time, arrange chicken on serving platter. Spoon sauce over chicken. Makes 6 servings.

DAUBE DE VOLAILLE
Chicken in Aspic

3-1/2 lb. chicken
4-1/4 cups water
salt
1 env. unflavored gelatine
1/4 cup water
4 tbs. butter
3 medium tomatoes
2 onions, chopped
2 carrots, sliced
1 clove garlic
3 shallots, chopped
1/2 cup port wine

The day before, remove legs and breast from chicken. Cut breast in half. Place back, wings, neck, liver, heart and gizzard in pot. Add 4 cups water and salt to taste. Simmer until stock has reduced to 2 cups. Strain. Soften gelatine in 1/4 cup cold water. Add to hot, strained broth. Stir to dissolve gelatine. Peel, seed and chop tomatoes. **While stock is reducing,** melt butter in large frying pan. Brown legs, thighs and breasts. Add onions, carrots, garlic through a press, shallots, tomatoes, port and stock with gelatine. Stir and season with additional salt and pepper if needed. Cook gently 1 hour. Remove chicken. Strain liquid and reserve vegetables. Skin and bone chicken. Cut meat into pieces. Place a layer of chicken on the bottom of a terrine. Cover with vegetables. Add strained stock. Cover and refrigerate overnight.

 Just before serving time, remove from refrigerator. Serve from the terrine. Makes 6 servings.

FOIE DE VOLAILLE MARIANNE
Chicken Livers with Mushrooms and Bacon

24 chicken livers
9 tbs. butter
2 ozs. shallots, chopped
1/2 cup red Burgundy wine
6 tbs. chicken broth

1 tsp. meat glaze
24 tiny mushroom caps
2 slices bacon, julienned
chopped parsley

In the late afternoon, cut livers in half. Melt 4 tablespoons butter in skillet. Cook livers gently until they turn pink. Remove from pan. Add shallots and Burgundy to same pan. Cook until liquid reduces one half. Stir in broth and meat glaze. In a separate pan melt 2 tablespoons butter. Add mushrooms and bacon. Cook until brown. Drain and add to sauce. Reduce by one half again. Lower heat until sauce is barely boiling. Add 3 tablespoons butter, a little at a time.

Just before serving time, dry livers and add to sauce. Shake pan to reheat livers without breaking them. Place livers and sauce in a small, deep bowl. Sprinkle with chopped parsley. Serve with French-fried potatoes. Makes 6 servings.

81

AIGUILETTES DE CANETON AU POMMARD
Breast of Duck with Red Wine

3 ducks (4 lbs. ea.)
10 tbs. butter
1 carrot, diced
2 onions, diced
3 tbs. flour
3 tbs. Cognac
1 bottle Pommard or
   red Burgundy
1-1/4 cups chicken broth

4 sprigs parsley
1/4 tsp. thyme
bay leaf
1 clove garlic
4 tsp. tomato paste
6 slices day-old bread
2 tbs. creme fraiche, page 4
1/4 tsp. potato flour
1 lb. tiny mushroom caps

Early in the day, remove the breasts from ducks. (Reserve legs for another use such as Pate De Canard Maison.) Retain the skin on the breasts. Cover breasts and refrigerate. Break up the remaining carcasses. Melt 4 tablespoons butter in a Dutch oven. Brown carcasses, carrots and onions. Add flour and cook 5 minutes. Pour Cognac over mixture and ignite. Add wine, broth, a bouquet garni consisting of parsley sprigs, thyme and bay leaf tied in a small piece of cheesecloth, garlic through a press, tomato paste, salt and pepper to taste. Cook slowly 2 hours or until nicely thickened. Strain and reserve. Cook mushroom caps in 2 tablespoons butter. Set aside.

About 25 minutes before serving time, place breasts skin side down in 4 tablespoons melted butter. Cook gently 15 minutes. Turn and cook 5 minutes longer. Remove from pan and keep hot. Brown bread slices on both sides in pan drippings. Pour off excess fat. Add cream fraiche and potato flour which have been mixed together. Add prepared duck sauce and correct seasonings. Arrange toast on a plate. Remove skin from breasts and cut in half. Slice each thinly but not quite all the way through. Arrange breasts on toast. Pour sauce over breasts. Garnish with mushroom caps. Makes 6 servings.

DINDONNEAU FARCI TOURANGELLE
Roast Turkey with Grape, Prune and Chicken Liver Stuffing

1/2 lb. Malaga grapes
6 tbs. port wine
5 chicken livers
24 pitted prunes
tea
1-1/2 lbs. sausage
13 lb. turkey
larding pork sheets
1/4 lb. butter
Mousseline Au Marrons, page 85

Early in the day, remove seeds from grapes. Soak grapes in port wine for 5 hours. Chop chicken livers. Cook prunes in tea to cover for 30 minutes. Drain prunes. Place sausage in bowl. Add grapes, port, prunes and chopped livers. Mix thoroughly. Cover and refrigerate. **About 3 hours before serving time,** season inside of turkey with salt and pep-

84

per. Put stuffing mixture into cavity. Cover breast only with a large piece of larding pork. Place turkey in roasting pan with butter. Roast in 350°F. oven 3 hours. Baste every 15 minutes and add 2 tablespoons water directly to the pan after each basting. Just before turkey is done, make Mousseline Au Marrons as directed.

When turkey is done, remove it to serving platter. Allow to rest. Deglaze the pan. Serve pan juices in separate dish.

Mousseline Au Marrons—Chestnut Puree

1-1/2 lbs. canned chestnuts
3/4 cup hot milk
3/4 cup creme fraiche, page 4
1/4 lb. butter

Run chestnuts through a meat grinder. Add milk, creme fraiche and butter. Whip until smooth. Keep hot in a double boiler over warm water. Press plastic wrap firmly against surface. Serve with turkey.

CANARD AU VERJUS
Roast Duck with Grape Stuffing, Apple Garnish

2 lbs. green apples
10 tbs. butter
sugar
5-6 lb. duck
1-1/2 lbs. seedless grapes
24 tiny white onions
2 tbs. Calvados
1/2 tsp. potato flour
5 ozs. creme fraiche, page 4

Early in the afternoon, peel and core apples. Cut into quarters. Lay in dish with 6 tablespoons melted butter. Sprinkle with sugar. Cook in 400°F. oven 30 minutes, turning often. Remove and set aside. **About one and a half hours before serving time,** season inside of duck with salt and pepper. Stuff with as many grapes as the cavity will hold. Sew up the opening. Prick surface of the duck all over with a fork. Melt 4 tablespoons butter in a Dutch oven. Brown duck slowly with onions. When well browned all over pour off excess

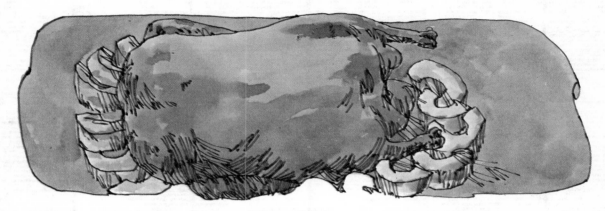

fat. Pour Calvados over duck and ignite. When flame goes out, cover Dutch oven and cook in 350°F. oven 1 hour and 15 minutes, or until duck tests done and juice runs clear when thigh is pierced with a fork.

At serving time, arrange duck on serving platter. Garnish with prepared apples. Keep warm. Drain excess fat from Dutch oven leaving 1 tablespoon. Mix potato flour and creme fraiche. Add to pan along with remaining grapes. Stir over medium heat until sauce boils and thickens. Serve separately. Makes 6 servings.

THE RIVIERA
FROM CROWDED
BEACHES
TO STEEP,
WINDING STREETS

M. NELSON
76

MEATS

The most popular entree served in our country is meat. The French, too, have a great liking for meat and fortunately for the do-it-ahead cook, there are more ways of preparing meat than perhaps any other item on the menu.

French cooking offers an infinite variety of meats, from the lesser cuts that often benefit by long slow braising or cooking, and variety cuts such as sweetbreads, kidneys and tongue, to classic rack of lamb and beef dishes.

I have tried here to present an assortment of recipes ranging from family style to elegant party type dishes that can be prepared by both adventurous and conservative cooks alike.

You will find that even the fanciest of recipes can be brought along the road to completion without a strain on the cook as the dinner hour approaches, if the prepare-ahead method is followed.

STEAK A LA TYROLIENNE
Filets with Tomato Sauce and Fried Onion Rings

4 large onions
1 lb. tomatoes
1 tbs. peanut oil
4 sprigs parsley
1/2 tsp. thyme
bay leaf
flour
deep fat for frying
6 filets mignon
5 tbs. butter

90

Early in the day, finely chop 1 onion. Peel, seed and finely chop tomatoes. Heat 1 tablespoon peanut oil and brown onion. Add tomatoes and a bouquet garni consisting of parsley, thyme and bay leaf tied in a small piece of cheesecloth. Cook over gentle heat 15 minutes, or until most of juice has cooked away. Season to taste with salt and pepper. Slice onions and separate into rings. Cover and set aside. **About 25 minutes before serving**

time, dredge onions in flour. Heat oil to 350°F. Fry onions until well browned. Drain and set aside on absorbent paper. Reheat tomato sauce and remove bouquet garni. Season steaks with salt and pepper. Melt 5 tablespoons butter in skillet over fairly high heat. Cook steaks 2 minutes on each side.

To serve, arrange steaks on heated plate. Place a spoonful of tomato sauce on each steak. Surround steaks with onion rings. Makes 6 servings.

Early
in the
day

TOURNEDOS AMBASSADRICE
Filets with Liver-Kidney Garnish and Madeira Sauce

6 slices day-old bread
18 tbs. butter
6 chicken livers
1 lamb kidney
12 button mushrooms
6 filets mignon
3 tbs. chicken broth
2 tbs. Madeira wine
1/2 tsp. tomato paste
1/4 tsp. potato flour

92

In the late afternoon, cut bread into rounds the size of the filets. Melt 4 tablespoons butter in skillet. Fry bread until golden on each side. Arrange on a round serving platter and set aside. Saute chicken livers briskly in 2 tablespoons butter until they are pink. Set aside. Cut kidney into small pieces and saute in 2 tablespoons very hot butter. Saute mushrooms in 2 tablespoons butter 15 minutes. Add to kidneys. Set aside.

Just before serving time, melt 4 tablespoons butter in a skillet. Cook filets over moderate heat 5 minutes on each side, or to taste. Reheat chicken livers while filets are cooking. Remove filets from pan and place on fried bread. Top filets with chicken livers. Place kidney mixture in the center of serving dish. Keep hot in a low oven. Add chicken broth to filet pan and reduce by half over high heat. Add Madeira, tomato paste, potato flour and 4 tablespoons butter. Reduce 2 minutes. Correct seasonings and spread some of the sauce over each filet. Serve immediately. Makes 6 servings.

HAMBURGER AU FROMAGE
French-Style Cheeseburgers

2 lbs. fat-free round steak, ground
4 shallots, chopped
2 tsp. parsley, chopped
1 tsp. paprika
1/2 tsp. powdered thyme
4 tsp. peanut oil
salt and pepper
6 slices Cheshire cheese
4 tbs. butter
2 onions, coarsely chopped
5 tbs. beef stock
4 tsp. catsup
1 tsp. Worcestershire sauce

In the afternoon, place freshly ground meat in a bowl. Add shallots, parsley, paprika, thyme, peanut oil, salt and pepper to taste. Mix lightly but thoroughly. Divide into 12 patties.

Place 1 slice of cheese on each of 6 patties. Cover with remaining patties. Seal edges well to contain cheese. Refrigerate.

About 30 minutes before serving time, melt butter in skillet. Brown patties about 10 minutes on one side. Add onion. Turn patties and brown 10 minutes longer. When cheeseburgers are done, arrange on a heated serving dish. Cover with onions. Add stock to pan. Boil 3 minutes. Stir in catsup and Worcestershire sauce. Correct seasoning and pour over cheeseburgers. Makes 6 servings.

BOEUF ARLESIENNE
Braised Beef Arles Style

4 tbs. peanut oil
2-1/2 lb. top sirloin or round steak, in one piece
2 large onions, coarsely chopped
2 carrots, finely chopped
3/4 cup chicken broth
6 tbs. white wine
1-1/4 lbs. tomatoes
3 ozs. green olives

In the early afternoon, heat oil in a Dutch oven. Brown meat well. Add onions, carrots, chicken broth and white wine. Cover and cook 2 hours in a 275°F. oven. **While meat is cooking,** peel, seed and chop tomatoes. Puree olives using a blender, if desired. Add tomatoes and olives to meat. Continue cooking 2 hours longer.

Just before serving time, remove meat from oven. Slice and arrange on a warm platter. Remove fat from top of sauce. Coat meat with sauce. Serve with spaghetti. Makes 6 servings.

BROCHETTE AGNEAU ET OIGNONS
Lamb and Onions on Skewers

Early in the day

3-1/2 lb. leg of lamb
2 cups peanut oil
juice of 2 lemons
1/2 lb. onions
2 tbs. bread crumbs

6 skewers
pieces of bay leaf
2 eggs
1 tsp. water

Early in the day, trim lamb and cut into 3/4-inch cubes. Combine oil and lemon juice in bowl. Add lamb cubes. Stir to coat well. Marinate until needed. Cut onion into pieces. Place in blender container. Cover and blend until pureed. Place onion puree in bowl. Add bread crumbs, salt and pepper to taste. **Shortly before serving time,** thread meat cubes onto skewers with a small piece of bay leaf between each piece. Brush meat with beaten egg. Roll in onion-bread crumb mixture.

Just before serving time, broil several minutes on each side or until meat is tender and well browned, but still pink on the inside. Serve immediately. Makes 6 servings.

NOTRE DAME
VIEW FROM LA TOUR D'ARGENT

M. NELSON

COTELETTES D'AGNEAU SEVIGNE
Baked Stuffed Lamb Chops

8 tbs. butter
2 ozs. shallots, chopped
1/2 lb. mushrooms, chopped
6 tbs. Chablis wine
salt and pepper
2 ozs. stale bread
3 egg yolks
12 small lamb rib chops (French lamb chops)
3 eggs
1 tsp. water
flour
bread crumbs

100

Early in the day, melt 4 tablespoons butter in Dutch oven. Add shallots and mushrooms. Pour in Chablis. Season with salt and pepper. Cook until all liquid has evaporated. Moisten stale bread with lukewarm water. Squeeze dry. Add to mushrooms.

Blend in egg yolks. Spread stuffing mixture on a plate. Cover surface tightly with plastic wrap. Refrigerate until well chilled. **In the afternoon,** salt and pepper lamb chops. Melt 2 tablespoons butter in skillet. Cook lamb chops 5 minutes on one side only. Turn cooked-side up. Spread with chilled stuffing. (If you keep your fingers moist, this task will be easy.) Beat eggs and water together. Dredge chops in flour. Spank to remove excess flour. Dip in egg then in bread crumbs. Remove excess crumbs. Arrange chops in buttered baking dish.

   About 15 minutes before serving time, melt remaining butter and brush over chops. Bake in 425°F. oven 15 minutes. If breading is not sufficiently browned, place chops under broiler until nicely browned and crisp. Makes 6 servings.

SELLE D'AGNEAU EN TERRINE
Saddle of Lamb in Aspic

5-1/2 lb. saddle of lamb, boned
salt and pepper
1 oz. truffles
1-1/2 tbs. Cognac
1 can <u>real</u> foie gras (not pate)
4 tbs. butter
1 cup port wine
2 env. unflavored gelatine
1-1/2 cups chicken broth

The night before, lay saddle of lamb out flat, skin side down. Season with salt and pepper. Cut truffles into chunks and sprinkle over meat. Then sprinkle with Cognac. Lightly cover and leave at room temperature overnight. **The next morning,** open the can of foie gras (very expensive but the resulting wonder is worth it) at both ends. Remove foie gras in one piece. Lay on marinated lamb and close meat over it. Tie the saddle closed. Melt butter in Dutch oven. Place lamb in pot. Cover and cook in 325°F. oven 1 hour. Add port. Continue cooking 15 minutes longer. When lamb is done, remove strings. Place lamb in a deep dish just large enough to hold it. Sprinkle gelatine over chicken broth and allow to soften. Heat mixture until gelatine completely dissolves. Degrease the liquid in which lamb cooked. Add half of it to gelatine mixture. Strain and pour over lamb until it is covered. Pour remaining aspic mixture into a flat dish. Refrigerate both dishes.

At serving time, unmold jellied lamb onto serving platter. Surround with the rest of aspic which has been finely chopped. Slice lamb into 1/2-inch slices. Serve with Salade Emilie, page 162. Makes 6 servings.

ECHINE DE PORC AU CELERI
Braised Pork Chops with Celery

12 (4 ozs. ea.) pork shoulder chops
salt and pepper
flour
4 tbs. butter
1 lb. celery
2 tsp. fresh rosemary or
   1/2 tsp. dried rosemary
1 large bottle red wine
4 sprigs parsley
1/2 tsp. thyme
bay leaf
2 tbs. creme fraiche, page 4

104

About 2 hours before serving time, salt and pepper chops. Dredge in flour and shake off excess. Heat butter in Dutch oven over moderate heat. Brown chops. Cut celery in pieces. Add to chops. Sprinkle with rosemary and stir in wine. Add a bouquet garni con-

sisting of parsley, thyme and bay leaf tied in a small piece of cheesecloth. Cook, uncovered, in 325°F. oven 1-1/2 hours.

Ten minutes before serving time, remove chops from oven. Allow fat to rise to top of sauce and remove. Pour sauce into large skillet and quickly reduce until it is slightly thicker than desired. Stir in creme fraiche. Arrange chops and celery on a deep platter. Pour sauce over chops. Serve with French fried potatoes. Makes 6 servings.

PORC A LA SAUGE
Roast Pork With Sage

4 tbs. butter
2-1/2 lb. boneless pork roast
2 tsp. fresh sage or
   1/2 tsp. dried sage
4 lumps sugar
6 tbs. red wine vinegar
3/4 cup chicken stock
juice of 1 orange

About two hours before serving time, heat butter in a Dutch oven over medium heat. Brown roast. Add sage, sugar, vinegar and chicken stock. Insert meat thermometer. Cook, uncovered, in 350ºF. oven 1 hour and 20 minutes, or until thermometer indicates pork is done. **Ten minutes before serving time,** add orange juice to roast. Return to oven for 10 minutes.

To serve, place roast on heated platter and surround with Carrots and Onions with Madeira, page 133. Degrease pan juices and serve on the side. Makes 6 servings.

THE LOUVRE

PORC AUX POMMES ET PRUNEAUX
Roast Pork Stuffed with Prunes, Apple Garnish

2-1/2 lb. boneless pork roast
6 ozs. pitted prunes
2-1/2 lbs. green apples
7 tbs. butter
1 cup chicken stock
red currant jelly

108

Early in the day, split roast almost in half, butterfly fashion (do not separate halves). Set aside. Place prunes in saucepan. Cover with cold water. Slowly bring to boil. Drain immediately and rinse with cold water. Dry prunes on paper toweling. Peel and core 1 pound of apples. Cut into quarters. Arrange apples and prunes on one half of roast. Close and tie roast. Refrigerate. Peel remaining apples. Cut in half crosswise and remove cores. Gently cook apples in 4 tablespoons butter, turning serveral times. Set aside. **About 2 hours before serving time,** melt remaining 3 tablespoons butter in Dutch oven. Brown roast thoroughly on all sides over moderate heat. Season with salt and pepper. Insert thermometer. Pour in stock. Place in 350°F. oven 1 hour and 30 minutes, turn meat every 20 minutes, or until thermometer indicates pork is done.

   At serving time, reheat apple halves and fill centers with currant jelly. Remove string from roast and place on a heated platter. Surround with jelly-filled apples. Degrease cooking juices and spoon some over roast. Serve remainder on the side. Makes 6 servings.

FILET PORC EN CROUTE
Pork Filet in Crust

2-1/2 lb. boneless pork roast
salt and pepper
1 pkg. Pepperidge Farm frozen patty shells
2 tsp. Dijon mustard
1 tsp. caraway seed
1 egg, beaten
110   7/8 cup chicken broth
1/2 tsp. potato flour

Early in the day, season pork with salt and pepper. Insert meat thermometer. Roast in a 350°F. oven 50 minutes, or until thermometer indicates meat is done. Remove from oven and chill. Do not wash roasting pan. Defrost patty shells. Press shells together and roll dough out large enough to encompass roast. Spread pastry with mustard. Sprinkle with caraway. Lay chilled roast on pastry. Wrap pastry tightly about meat and seal well. Prick in several places to allow steam to escape. Brush pastry with beaten egg. Set aside. Add 3/4-cup broth to roasting pan. Mix well and strain. Let grease rise and skim it off.

About 35 minutes before serving time, bake pastry-wrapped roast in 375°F. oven 30 minutes. Dissolve potato flour in remaining 2 tablespoons stock. Stir into strained broth. Bring to a boil and simmer 5 minutes. Slice roast at the table. Pass sauce. Makes 6 servings.

JAMBONNEAU DE PORC AU BEAUJOLAIS
Braised Fresh Ham with Beaujolais

4 ozs. carrots
6 ozs. onions
2 ozs. mushrooms
1 stalk celery
2 cloves garlic
8 tbs. butter
2-1/2 tbs. flour
1 large bottle Beaujolais
4 tsp. tomato paste

4 sprigs parsley
1/2 tsp. thyme
bay leaf
3/4 cup bouillon
1 tsp. meat glaze
1/2 fresh ham, shank end
2-1/2 lbs. potatoes
chopped parsley

112

Early in the day, finely chop carrots, onions, mushrooms and celery. Put garlic through a press. Melt butter in Dutch oven. Add vegetables and garlic. Brown well. Add flour and cook 5 minutes. Gradually stir in Beaujolaise. Blend well. Add tomato paste, a bouquet garni consisting of parsley, thyme and bay leaf tied in a small piece of cheesecloth, bouillon and meat glaze. Set aside. **About 2-1/2 hours before serving time,** bring sauce to boil. Add ham. Cover and cook in 325°F. oven 2-1/2 hours. **About 1-3/4 hours before ser-**

ving time, prepare steamed potatoes (Pommes Vapeur). Peel potatoes. Cut in half or quarters if very large. Arrange on a rack over boiling water or in a steamer. Cover pot and steam potatoes 1-1/2 hours.

    To serve, arrange ham on serving platter. Place steamed potatoes around ham. Sprinkle potatoes with chopped parsley. Strain sauce and serve it separately. Makes 6 servings.

ESCALOPE DE VEAU RONSARD
Spinach-Stuffed Veal with Madeira Sauce

2 lbs. veal steaks
1-3/4 lbs. tomatoes
14 tbs. butter
salt, pepper, pinch sugar
2 lbs. fresh spinach
1 qt. boiling water
4 ozs. Gruyere cheese, diced
4 tbs. Madeira wine
6 tbs. chicken broth
2 tsp. potato flour
6 tbs. creme fraiche, page 4

114

Early in the day, remove edges and gristle from veal. Place pieces between sheets of waxed paper. Pound until very thin. If necessary, overlap some of pieces. Pound them together until you have formed 6 large, thin pieces. Leave meat between waxed paper sheets and refrigerate. Peel, seed and chop tomatoes to a paste. Melt 4 tablespoons butter in heavy skillet. Cook tomatoes until all moisture has evaporated. (This is called tomato con-cassee.) Season with salt, pepper and a pinch of sugar. Set aside. Wash spinach well and remove stems. Cook in boiling, salted water 5 minutes. Drain and rinse with cold water. Squeeze to remove excess moisture. Melt 2 tablespoons butter in pot. Cook spinach in butter 5 minutes. Add diced Gruyere. Divide spinach mixture equally between the 6 pieces of veal. Fold meat to completely enclose filling. Tie veal birds with string.

About 25 minutes before serving time, heat 8 tablespoons butter in skillet. Brown veal about 10 minutes on each side. Reheat tomato concassee. Arrange veal birds on ser-ving plate. Place a spoonful of tomato concassee on each piece of meat. Add Madeira to skillet and ignite. When flame goes out, add chicken broth. Combine flour and creme fraiche. Add to skillet. Stir until sauce boils. Simmer 1 minute. Strain over meat. Makes 6 servings.

COTES DE VEAU VIGNERONNE
Veal Chops with Tomatoes, Curry and Grapes

6 veal rib chops
salt and pepper
6 tbs. butter
2 tomatoes
1 tsp. curry powder
1/2 tsp. potato flour
6 tbs. creme fraiche, page 4
10 ozs. seedless grapes

117

In the late afternoon, season chops with salt and pepper. Melt butter in a skillet over moderate heat. Cook chops 10 minutes, turning once or twice. While chops are cooking, peel, seed and chop tomatoes. Add tomatoes and curry to chops. Stir and set aside.

About 15 minutes before serving time, return chops to moderate heat and cook 10 minutes. Remove chops from pan and arrange on a warm serving platter. Keep warm. Combine potato flour and creme fraiche. Add to pan along with grapes. Bring to boil and simmer until sauce thickens. Correct seasoning and spread over chops. Makes 6 servings.

PAUPIETTES DE VEAU LOCHOISE
Veal Birds with Foie Gras and Mushroom Sauce

6 veal steaks
1/4 lb. thinly sliced Prosciutto
4-1/2 ozs. _real_ foie gras
6 sheets larding pork
10 tbs. butter
2 tbs. flour
2 cups milk
3 tbs. creme fraiche, page 4
salt and pepper
1-1/4 lbs. mushrooms
6 tbs. dry white wine
6 slices day-old bread

118

Early in the day, trim edges and gristle from veal. Pound between sheets of waxed paper in such a way as to create 6 large, very thin slices of veal. Cover veal slices with Prosciutto. Pound again lightly to weld the Prosciutto to the veal. Cut foie gras into 6 fingers.

Place one on each piece of meat. Fold in sides and roll to enclose foie gras. Wrap each roll (paupiette) in a sheet of larding pork. Tie with string. **About an hour before serving time,** melt 2 tablespoons butter in a heavy saucepan. Stir in flour. Remove from heat and blend in milk and creme fraiche. Return to heat and stir until sauce boils. Reduce heat to low. Simmer gently 30 minutes. Stir occasionally. Season with salt and pepper. Grind mushrooms and add to sauce. Cook 10 minutes longer. **About half an hour before serving time,** heat 4 tablespoons butter in skillet. Brown paupiettes slowly. Add salt, pepper and wine. Simmer 25 minutes. Turn occasionally.

Just before serving, melt remaining 4 tablespoons butter in skillet. Brown bread slices on both sides. Place on platter. Arrange a paupiette on each slice. Surround with sauce. Makes 6 servings.

COTES DE VEAU SURPRISE
Mock Veal Chops

1-1/2 lbs. tender fat-free veal
6 small rib <u>bones</u> (ask butcher)
5 ozs. stale bread
3/4 cup milk
salt and pepper
2-1/2 lbs. carrots
18 tbs. butter
4 cups chicken stock

120

Early in the day, put veal through the coarse blade of a meat grinder. Wash and dry bones and set aside. Soak bread in milk and squeeze dry. Place ground veal in bowl with 10 tablespoons soft, not melted, butter, soaked bread, salt and pepper. Mix gently but thoroughly. Divide mixture into 6 equal portions. Shape each to resemble a veal chop. Insert a bone into each chop to complete the resemblance. Cover and refrigerate. Peel and thinly slice carrots. Melt 4 tablespoons butter in saucepan. Add carrots and chicken stock. Season with salt and pepper. Bring to boil and cook, uncovered, over moderate heat 40 minutes, or

until nearly all liquid has evaporated. Set aside. **About 20 minutes before serving time,** melt remaining 4 tablespoons butter in large skillet. Cook "chops" 10 minutes on each side. Reheat carrots.

To serve, place carrots in center of a heated serving dish. Arrange "chops" around carrots and coat them with the butter in which they cooked. Makes 6 servings.

LANGUE AUX NOIX DE CAJOU
Beef Tongue with Cashew Nuts

1 tongue, fresh or corned
1 carrot, sliced
1 stalk celery, sliced
2 leeks, sliced
4 sprigs parsley
1/2 tsp. thyme
bay leaf
2 cups cooking broth
5 ozs. dry-roasted cashews
3 tbs. butter
1-1/2 tbs. flour
1 egg yolk
3/4 cup creme fraiche, page 4
juice of 1 lemon

122

The day before, place tongue in a pot with 3 quarts water. Add salt if tongue is fresh. Add carrot, celery, leeks and bouquet garni consisting of parsley, thyme and bay leaf tied in a small piece of cheesecloth. Simmer over low heat until tongue is tender, about 3 hours. Remove tongue and reserve 2 cups cooking broth. Rinse tongue in cold water. Remove skin and slice tongue. Wrap tightly and refrigerate. **Early the next day,** melt butter in saucepan over moderate heat. Stir in flour. Gradually blend in cooking broth. Stir until sauce boils. Beat egg yolk into creme fraiche. Add a little of the hot sauce, then add mixture to sauce. Stir in lemon juice. Cover with plastic wrap pressed firmly against surface and refrigerate.

Shortly before serving time, reheat sauce to cook egg yolks, but do not boil. Melt 3 tablespoons butter in large skillet. Saute tongue slices gently 2 to 3 minutes on each side. Arrange slices overlapping on a heated platter. Sprinkle with nuts and coat with sauce. Makes 6 servings.

RIZ DE VEAU EN GELEE
Sweetbreads In Aspic

2 lbs. sweetbreads
juice of 1 lemon
salt
2 onions
2 carrots
6 shallots
1 clove garlic
2 tbs. butter
1 oz. whole truffles
1 cup port wine
1 cup bouillon
1 env. unflavored gelatine
1/4 cup water

The night before, place sweetbreads in a pan with lemon juice and a little salt. Cover with cold water. Bring slowly to a boil. Simmer gently 10 minutes. Drain and plunge into ice water. Handling carefully, remove fat, skin and gristle. Place sweetbreads between two plates. Weigh down with a heavy object. Leave this way and refrigerate overnight. **Early in the day,** coarsely chop onions, carrots and shallots. Put garlic through a press. Melt butter in a skillet. Add sweetbreads and cook gently 5 minutes on each side. Add truffles, onions, carrots, shallots, garlic, port and bouillon. Cook slowly over gentle heat 1 hour. Remove sweetbreads and truffles. Strain liquid. Soften gelatine in 1/4-cup water. Add to hot liquid. Stir until gelatine is melted. Cut sweetbreads and truffles into fine strips. Place in a terrine. Add liquid and refrigerate until set.

At **serving time,** remove from refrigerator and serve from the terrine. Makes 6 servings.

125

PICKING A
PAINTING ON THE
STREETS OF PARIS

M. NELSON 76

VEGETABLES

If there is any room left on my heart after inscribing the phrase, "Can I cook it ahead?", I am sure that investigators will find right along side it the words, "Please give me a new way of preparing vegetables!" Like Sisyphus, the mythological Greek, who spent his life pushing a heavy rock uphill only to have it plunge recklessly once again to the bottom, it seems that I can never finally achieve that moment when my students' quest for vegetable recipes will be satisfied, and that is why this section of this volume is lengthier than most of the others. But even as I write this, I know it is only a stop-gap and the search will go on forever.

Yet, these recipes are, in the main, different and intriguing and, best of all, they fit wonderfully into the pattern of getting things done ahead of time. Some of the dishes here will serve admirably as accompaniments to the meat and fish recipes, and others can stand alone, or as adjuncts to a buffet meal. None of them will strain your patience or your preserverance, nor will your guests regret their presence on the table.

ARTICHAUT CAVOUR
Tiny Artichokes with Cheese and Hard-Cooked Eggs

36 tiny artichokes
6 cups boiling water
juice of 1 lemon
9 tbs. butter
4 ozs. grated imported Parmesan cheese
1/4 cup chopped parsley
2 hard-cooked eggs, finely chopped

In the afternoon, trim tough outer leaves from artichokes. Cut off tops and bottoms to make the hearts resemble the ones which come in cans. Cook in boiling, salted water with lemon juice added for 25 minutes. Drain and dry on paper toweling. Barely melt 7 tablespoons butter in small casserole. One by one dip the artichokes in butter. Then roll in Parmesan. Arrange in a flameproof serving dish. Dot with 2 tablespoons butter. Set aside.

Just before serving, place under broiler to brown. Sprinkle with chopped parsley and finely chopped eggs. Makes 6 to 8 servings.

5 lbs. fresh asparagus
3 eggs
6 tbs. milk
1/2 tsp. salt

1 cup flour
7 ozs. Prosciutto, finely chopped
2 ozs. grated Parmesan cheese

Early in the day, snap tips from asparagus. Cook them according to the Paul Mayer Method on page 5. Trim the cooked tips to 3-inch lengths. Set aside. Place 2 eggs, milk, salt and flour in blender container. Cover and blend until mixture becomes a heavy batter. Using a crepe pan or skillet make 6 5-inch crepes. Set aside. Combine chopped ham with remaining egg. Butter a flat, round, ovenproof platter. Lay one crepe on bottom of platter. Spread 1/5 of the ham mixture on crepe. Arrange 1/5 of the asparagus tips on ham. Cover with another crepe and continue in this fashion until everything has been used. Make an attractive design on the top crepe with the asparagus. Sprinkle with Parmesan. Cover and set aside.

About 25 minutes before serving time, place tart in 350°F. oven. Bake 20 minutes. Cut into 6 wedges like a pie. Serve immediately. Makes 6 servings.

129

CHOUX BRUXELLES AUX MARRONS
Brussels Sprouts and Chestnuts

4 cups oil
1 lb. chestnuts
7 tbs. butter
4 cups bouillon
1 tsp. meat glaze
salt and pepper
1-1/2 lbs. Brussels sprouts
3/4 cup creme fraiche, page 4
2 tsp. potato flour

130

Early in the day, heat oil to 350°F. in a large pot. Make a criss-cross on the flat side of each chestnut. Drop chestnuts into hot oil. Cook 10 minutes. Lift from oil. When cool enough to handle remove peeling. Melt butter in a flat baking dish. Add chestnuts, bouillon and meat glaze. Season with salt, if needed, and pepper. Place, uncovered, in 375°F. oven 25 minutes. **While chestnuts are in the oven,** trim Brussels sprouts and cook according to the Paul Mayer Method on page 5. Drain well. Remove chestnuts from oven. Add

Brussels sprouts. Beat creme fraiche and potato flour together. Gently combine with chestnuts and sprouts. Cover and refrigerate. **About an hour before serving time,** remove dish from refrigerator and let stand at room temperature until time to finish baking.

  About 25 minutes before serving time, place in 375ºF. oven. Bake 20 minutes or until thoroughly heated. Makes 6 servings.

CHOUX ROUGE FLAMANDE
Red Cabbage Flemish Style

1 large red cabbage
7 tbs. butter
6 tbs. red wine vinegar
salt and pepper
6 small green apples
2 tbs. sugar

In the afternoon, cut cabbage into quarters, remove the core and shred. Melt butter in a Dutch oven. Add vinegar, cabbage, salt and pepper to taste. Cover and cook over low heat 1 hour. Peel, core and cut apples into chunks. Add apples and sugar to cabbage. Mix gently. Remove from heat and set aside.

About 1 hour before serving time, cover cabbage and cook in 325°F. oven 1 hour. Makes 6 servings.

CARROTES AU MADERE
Carrots and Onions with Madeira

2-1/4 lbs. carrots
12 tiny onions
5 ozs. bacon
4 tbs. butter
salt and pepper

4 sprigs parsley
1/2 tsp. thyme
bay leaf
6 tbs. Madeira wine
chopped parsley

In the afternoon, peel carrots and onions. Cut carrots into thick slices. Cut bacon into short strips. Place in small saucepan and cover with cold water. Bring just to the boiling point. Drain bacon and rinse with cold water. Melt butter in a small Dutch oven. Add carrots and onions. Cook until nicely browned. Season with salt and pepper. Tie parsley, thyme and bay leaf in a small piece of cheesecloth. Add to vegetables along with bacon and Madeira. Set aside.

About 40 minutes before serving time, cover vegetables. Gently cook over low heat 35 minutes. Stir vegetables once or twice to prevent sticking. Remove bouquet garni.

At serving time, place carrots and onions in serving dish and sprinkle with parsley. Makes 6 servings.

133

CELERI AU GRATIN
Braised Celery with Cheese

6 small bunches celery
5 qts. water
11 tbs. butter
4 ozs. carrots, sliced
4 ozs. onions, sliced
salt and pepper
4 sprigs parsley
1/2 tsp. thyme
bay leaf
8 cups beef stock
3/4 lb. larding pork
5 ozs. grated Parmesan cheese

134

In the afternoon, wash celery well with vegetable brush. Leave whole but trim off all the leaves. Place celery in a large kettle with water. Add salt. Bring to a boil. Reduce heat and cook gently 15 minutes. Drain and rinse with cold water. Melt 7 tablespoons butter in a

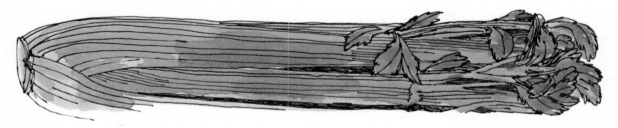

Dutch oven. Add carrots and onions. Cook gently 10 minutes without taking on any color. Cut celery bunches in half lengthwise. Lay on top of carrots and onions. Add salt, pepper, a bouquet garni consisting of parsley, thyme and bay leaf tied in a small piece of cheesecloth, and stock. Cut larding pork in thin flat slices. Cover the surface of celery and stock completely with pork slices. Set aside.

About one and one half hours before serving time, cover the pot and cook in 350°F. oven 1 hour and 15 minutes. Remove from oven and arrange the celery on a flameproof serving dish. Sprinkle celery with Parmesan and drizzle 4 tablespoons melted butter over all. Place under broiler 5 minutes. Serve immediately. Makes 6 servings.

Note: Save the delicious juices for making soups and sauces. Chill and remove fat, then refrigerate or freeze until needed.

CROQUETTES DE CHOUFLEUR
Cauliflower Croquettes

1-3/4 lbs. cauliflower
2 tbs. butter
5 tbs. flour
2 cups milk

salt and pepper
2 ozs. Gruyere cheese
deep fat for frying
fine bread crumbs

Early in the day, wash cauliflower and break into flowerets. Cook in boiling, salted water 5 minutes. Drain and set aside. Melt butter in saucepan. Add flour and cook gently, stirring, 5 minutes. Remove from heat and gradually blend in milk. Season with salt and pepper. Stir sauce with a wire whip over low heat until it boils. Cook gently 30 minutes, stirring occasionally. Add cheese and cook 5 minutes longer. Dredge cauliflower lightly in flour. Dip pieces into hot sauce and arrange on a rack or platter to chill.

Just before serving time, heat deep fat to 325°F. Roll chilled cauliflower in fine bread crumbs. Fry in hot fat until nicely browned. Drain on absorbent paper. Serve hot. Makes 6 servings.

136

AUBERGINES DUXELLOISE
Eggplant Stuffed with Mushrooms

Early
in the
day

3 small eggplants
7 tbs. butter
5 ozs. onions, chopped
7 ozs. mushrooms, chopped

6 tbs. Chablis wine
salt and pepper
1 egg yolk
1 oz. stale bread

Early in the day, cut eggplants in half lengthwise. With a sharp knife or curved grapefruit knife, cut around center of eggplants leaving the shells about 1/2-inch thick. Do not remove the loosened center. Place eggplants in lightly greased baking dish. Bake in 350°F. oven 10 minutes. Remove from oven and cool. **While eggplants are cooling,** melt 4 tablespoons butter in skillet. Cook onions slowly until golden. Add mushrooms, Chablis, salt and pepper. Cook rapidly 10 minutes or until liquid has evaporated. Remove from heat. Add egg yolk and bread which has been soaked in warm water and squeezed dry. Mix well. Remove loosened centers from baked eggplant halves. Chop and add to stuffing. Fill shells with stuffing. Cover and set aside.

About 45 minutes before serving time, melt remaining butter. Drizzle over stuffed eggplants. Bake in 350°F. oven 40 minutes. Serve immediately. Makes 6 servings.

137

COMPOTE D'AUBERGINES
Eggplant Casserole

1-3/4 lb. eggplant	1 lb. <u>each</u> tomatoes and mushrooms
6 tbs. oil	2-1/4 cups chicken broth
12 tbs. butter	2 ozs. dry bread crumbs
salt and pepper	2 ozs. grated Parmesan cheese

138

Early in the day, peel eggplant and cut into fine dice. Heat 3 tablespoons oil and 4 tablespoons butter in skillet. Cook eggplant until golden. Season with salt and black pepper. Keep hot. Peel, seed and slice tomatoes. Cook slices in 4 tablespoons butter until all moisture has evaporated. Season. Heat 3 more tablespoons oil and 4 tablespoons butter until very hot. Cook mushrooms until well browned and moisture has evaporated. Season. Butter an ovenproof terrine or loaf pan. Place a layer of eggplant on bottom. Top with layer of tomato slices. Add a layer of mushrooms. Repeat layers, finishing with mushrooms on top. Heat broth and pour over vegetables. Combine bread crumbs and Parmesan. Sprinkle over top. Bake in 325°F. oven 1-1/4 hours. Cool and refrigerate.

At serving time, slice chilled loaf. Serve cold. Makes 6 servings.

M. NELSON

ENDIVES A LA ROYALE
Endives Baked in Custard

1-1/4 lbs. Belgin endives
7 tbs. butter
juice of 1 lemon
1-1/2 tbs. water
6 tbs. creme fraiche, page 4
3 eggs

140

Early in the day, wash and dry endives. Melt 4 tablespoons butter in a Dutch oven. Arrange endives in the butter. Add lemon juice and water. Season to taste with salt and pepper. Cover the pot and cook 25 minutes in 350°F. oven. Remove from oven and drain. Dry endives on absorbent paper. Melt 3 tablespoons butter in an ovenproof serving dish. Arrange endives in butter. Cover and set aside. Beat creme fraiche and eggs together. Season with salt and pepper. Cover and refrigerate.

About 25 minutes before serving time, pour custard over endives. Bake in 375°F. oven 20 minutes or until custard is set and nicely browned. Makes 6 servings.

HARICOTS VERTS AU BACON
Green Beans with Bacon

Early in the day

2-1/2 lbs. green beans
5 ozs. bacon
7 tbs. butter
chopped parsley

Early in the day, wash beans. Remove tips and strings. Cook beans whole according to the Paul Mayer Method on page 5. Drain and cut crosswise into small pieces. Cut bacon into fine dice. Melt butter in a large skillet or Dutch oven. Add bacon and cook 5 minutes. Add beans and mix well. Set aside.

About 15 minutes before serving time, cook beans over very low heat 10 minutes longer. Serve sprinkled with parsley. Makes 6 servings.

141

OIGNONS FARCIS
Stuffed Onions

6 large onions
2 qts. water
5 ozs. mushrooms
8 tbs. butter

4 ozs. stale bread
2 egg yolks
2 cups beef stock
1 oz. grated Parmesan cheese

Early in the day, remove the bottom root ends from onions. Do not cut off tops. Cook onions in boiling salted water 15 minutes. Carefully hollow out centers leaving a shell about 1/4-inch thick. Chop onion centers and mushrooms together. Melt 4 tablespoons butter in skillet. Cook onion-mushroom mixture 20 minutes or until all liquid has evaporated. Season with salt and pepper. Soak bread in lukewarm water and squeeze dry. Add bread and egg yolks to onion-mushroom mixture. Mix well and stuff into onions. Butter a baking dish with 4 tablespoons butter and arrange onions in dish. Cover and set aside.

About one half hour before serving time, pour beef stock around onions. Bake in 350ºF. oven 30 minutes. Remove onions to flameproof serving dish. Pour juices into saucepan. Place over high heat and reduce to half. Sprinkle Parmesan over onions and place under broiler to brown tops. Pass reduced juices separately. Makes 6 servings.

POMMES DE TERRE BYRON
Baked Creamed Potato Patties

Early
in the
day

2-1/4 lbs. potatoes
12 tbs. butter
salt and pepper
1-1/2 tbs. chopped chives
3/4 cup creme fraiche, page 4
4 ozs. Gruyere cheese, grated

143

Early in the day, peel potatoes and cut into chunks. Cook in boiling, salted water 20 minutes. Drain well and force through a Foley food mill or ricer. Add butter and season with salt and pepper. Add chives. Spread mixture in foil-lined flat pan. Chill thoroughly. When chilled, turn the potato mixture out onto a lightly floured surface. Cut and shape mixture into 6 equal-sized patties. Butter 6 individual baking dishes. Place a patty in each dish. Cover and set aside.

About 15 minutes before serving time, heat creme fraiche and pour it equally over patties. Sprinkle with cheese. Place under hot broiler 10 minutes. Makes 6 servings.

POMMES DE TERRE LORETTE
Deep-Fried Potato Puffs

2-1/4 lbs. potatoes
1 egg
4 egg yolks
7 tbs. butter
4 ozs. Gruyere cheese
1 cup water
10 tbs. butter
1 cup <u>plus</u> 2 tbs. flour
4 eggs
deep fat for frying

In the afternoon, cook potatoes in boiling salted water in a covered pot 20 minutes. Drain and return pot to high heat to remove all moisture from potatoes. Shake pan constantly to avoid scorching. Force potatoes through a Foley food mill or other pureeing device. Beat in egg and egg yolks. Add butter and Gruyere. Set aside. Place water, butter and a little salt in a deep, heavy saucepan. Bring to boil. When mixture is boiling, add flour all at once.

Remove from heat and beat mixture rapidly with a heavy wooden spoon until it forms a shiny ball and leaves the sides of pan. Add eggs one at a time. Beat at least 30 seconds after each addition. This is best done with an electric mixer. Continue beating at least one minute after adding the last egg. Combine with potato mixture. Mix thoroughly. Set aside.

Just before serving, drop mixture by spoonfuls into hot fat 380ºF. Cook until puffed and crisp. Drain on absorbent paper. Sprinkle with salt. Serve immediately, as puffs become soggy if held. Makes 6 servings.

POMMES DE TERRE A LA MENTHE
Creamed Minted Potatoes

2 tbs. butter
1 cup <u>plus</u> 2 tbs. creme fraiche, page 4
1/2 tsp. dried mint <u>or</u>
   4 tsp. fresh mint, chopped
salt and pepper
2-1/4 lbs. potatoes

146

Early in the day, melt butter in a saucepan. Beat together creme fraiche and potato flour. Stir into melted butter. Add mint, salt and pepper. Gently stir over moderate heat until sauce thickens and boils. Pour into bowl. Cover with plastic wrap pressed firmly against surface. Refrigerate.

About half an hour before serving time, peel potatoes and cut into 1/2-inch cubes. Cook in boiling salted water about 20 minutes. **While potatoes are cooking,** slowly reheat sauce and allow to simmer gently 5 minutes, stirring occasionally. Drain potatoes well and return to heat to remove excess moisture. Shake pan to prevent scorching. Place potatoes in serving dish. Pour sauce over potatoes and serve immediately. Makes 6 servings.

POMMES DE TERRE SURPRISE
Baked Stuffed Potatoes

6 large Idaho or Russet potatoes
3 egg yolks
3 ozs. ham, finely diced
12 tbs. butter
salt and pepper
2 ozs. grated Parmesan cheese
butter for dotting

147

Early in the day, scrub potatoes. Dry and rub skins with oil. Prick each potato several places to allow steam to escape as they bake. Bake in 350°F. oven 45 minutes. Remove from oven and cut a lengthwise slice from top of each potato. Scoop out potato pulp leaving the shell intact. Combine potato, egg yolks, ham and butter. Season with salt and freshly ground pepper. Stuff shells with mixture. Cover with plastic wrap and refrigerate. **About an hour before baking,** remove from refrigerator and bring to room temperature.

About twenty minutes before serving time, sprinkle each potato with Parmesan and dot with butter. Bake in 375°F. oven 15 minutes, or until nicely crusted and browned. Makes 6 servings.

ROYALE D'EPINARDS
Spinach Custard with Hollandaise

2-1/2 lbs. fresh spinach
6 eggs
6 tbs. creme fraiche, page 4
1/2 tsp. potato flour
salt and pepper
12 tbs. butter
2 egg yolks
2 tbs. cream
1 tsp. lemon juice
salt and white pepper

148

In the afternoon, trim stems from spinach. Cook leaves in boiling, salted water 15 minutes. Drain and rinse thoroughly in cold water. Squeeze leaves a few at a time to extract as much moisture as possible. Force spinach through Foley food mill or other pureeing device. Place pureed spinach in skillet. Return to heat to evaporate any remaining moisture. Beat eggs with creme fraiche and potato flour. Combine with spinach and season highly with salt and freshly ground pepper. Cover with plastic pressed against surface of mixture. Refrigerate. **About 2 hours before serving time,** place 8 tablespoons butter, egg yolks, cream, lemon juice, salt and white pepper in heavy saucepan. Stir over low heat until sauce thickens. Do not let boil. Transfer to bowl and cover with plastic pressed firmly against surface of sauce. Set aside.

    About one half an hour before serving time, butter 6 individual souffle dishes using 4 tablespoons butter. Fill dishes with spinach mixture. Place in shallow pan and surround with boiling water. Cook in 350ºF. oven 20 minutes, or until knife inserted in center comes out clean. Remove from oven. Allow to rest a minute, then unmold onto a round serving platter. Coat with Hollandaise sauce. Brown quickly under heated broiler. Makes 6 servings.

FLAN DE TOMATE
Tomato Tart

1-3/4 cups flour	6 tbs. creme fraiche, page 4
1/4 tsp. salt	1/2 tsp. paprika
7 tbs. butter	1 lb. tomatoes
3 tbs. ice water	salt and pepper
3 eggs	

150

Early in the day, combine flour and salt in mixing bowl. Cut in butter with pastry blender until mixture resembles fine meal. Sprinkle water over mixture. Blend by tossing lightly with a fork until dough gathers into a ball. Let rest 1 hour. Roll dough out and line an 8- or 9-inch tart pan. Prick all over the surface with a fork. Bake in 300°F. oven 15 minutes. (Shell will be slightly underbaked.) Cool on rack. Beat eggs, creme fraiche and paprika together. Refrigerate. Peel, seed and squeeze all juice from tomatoes. Turn upside down to drain well.

About one half hour before serving time, cut tomatoes into chunks. Place in partly baked shell. Season with salt and pepper. Pour custard mixture over tomatoes. Bake tart in 350°F. oven 20 minutes or until custard has set, puffed and is nicely browned on top. Makes 6 servings.

NAVETS AU JUS
Simmered Turnips

In the after-noon

2-1/4 lbs. white turnips
7 tbs. butter, melted
1 tsp. meat glaze (Bovril)
4 cups beef stock
salt and pepper

4 sprigs parsley
1/2 tsp. thyme
bay leaf
chopped parsley <u>or</u>
   3 ozs. raisins, soaked 1 hour

In the afternoon, peel turnips and cut into 3/4 inch cubes. Place in pot. Cover with cold water and bring to a boil. Simmer gently 5 minutes. Drain and rinse with cold water. Place turnips in a Dutch oven with melted butter. Add meat glaze, broth, salt (if needed) and black pepper. Add a bouquet garni consisting of parsley, thyme and bay leaf tied in a small piece of cheesecloth. Stir mixture and set aside.

About 45 minutes before serving time, bring turnips to boil. Reduce heat and simmer, uncovered, 40 minutes, or until liquid has nearly evaporated and is thick enough to coat the turnips. Serve sprinkled with parsley or well-drained raisins. Makes 6 servings.

151

UNDERGOING
NEW PAINT AT LOW
TIDE IN THE HARBOR OF
ST. JEAN-DE-LUZ

M. NELSON 76

SALADS

Most salads can be made ahead, however in the case of mixed greens or a simple leaf salad, the dressing should be added just before serving because the crispness of fresh lettuce is destroyed by prolonged contact with oil and vinegar. There are many other types of salad, however, which can benefit from marination, and still others which require molding and need several hours in the refrigerator in order to set properly.

In my opinion, the proper place for a lettuce salad is between the main course and dessert, and not at the beginning of the meal where it so frequently appears. Not so for salads of meat or vegetables! These can serve as first courses, or accompanied by hot breads they will do admirably as principal dishes for a simple luncheon, or even a hot weather evening meal.

One nice feature about the first course or main dish salad is the fact that a wide variety of foods can be used to create it, and this can prove to be an easy method for using up those small quantities left in the refrigerator. The range of salad ideas is limited only by the imagination, and those offered here are but a few of the many which can be achieved.

SALADE BEAU SOLEIL
Apple-Rice Salad with Curried Mayonnaise

7 ozs. (1 cup) rice
2 qts. boiling water
20 roasted hazelnuts
3/4 cup mayonnaise
1 tsp. curry powder
16 pitted black olives, sliced
6 small green apples

Early in the day, cook rice in boiling, salted water 20 minutes. Drain and rinse with cold water. Drain thoroughly. Cover and refrigerate. Wash lettuce. Drain and dry, then cut into 6 wedges. Wrap and refrigerate. Peel hazelnuts and split in half. Mix mayonnaise, curry powder, half of hazelnuts and half of the olives. Cover and refrigerate. **An hour or so before serving time,** peel apples and cut into wedges. Cover with water and refrigerate.

Just before serving time, drain and dry apples. Place rice in center of platter. Make a crown of apple wedges on top of rice. Coat with mayonnaise. Arrange lettuce wedges around the base. Decorate top of salad with remaining hazelnuts and olives. Makes 6 servings.

SALADE AMUSANTE
Beef-Cheese-Ham Salad with Roquefort Dressing

2 tbs. red wine vinegar
6 tbs. peanut oil
1/2 tsp. paprika
2 ozs. Roquefort cheese
salt and pepper
4 ozs. Gouda cheese

4 ozs. ham
5 ozs. cooked beets
15 pitted ripe olives
1-1/4 lbs. Belgin endives
chopped chives

155

In the afternoon, combine vinegar, oil, paprika, Roquefort, salt and pepper. Blend together well. Cut Gouda, ham and well-drained beets into small dice. Slice olives crosswise. Combine cheese, ham, beets and olives with dressing. Refrigerate. Wash and dry endives. Separate into individual leaves. Refrigerate in plastic bags.

Just before serving time, arrange endive leaves on 6 individual salad plates. Spoon chilled mixture over leaves. Sprinkle with chopped chives. Makes 6 servings.

SALAD ROSE
Molded Beet and Potato Salad with Tomato Mayonnaise

1-3/4 lbs. potatoes
3/4 lb. fresh beets
1 env. unflavored gelatine
6 tbs. bouillon
salt and pepper
2 tbs. red wine vinegar
6 tbs. peanut oil
2 tsp. Dijon mustard
1-1/4 cups mayonnaise
2 tsp. tomato paste
4 carrots, shredded
black olive slices
watercress

Early in the day, peel potatoes and cut into chunks. Cook in boiling, salted water 25 minutes. Cook unpeeled beets in boiling, salted water 25 minutes. Drain beets and slip off skins. Drain potatoes and return to brisk heat to remove excess moisture. Shake pan to prevent scorching. Force beets and potatoes through Foley food mill or other pureeing device. Mix together well. Soften gelatine in bouillon. Heat gently to dissolve gelatine. Cool over cold water but do not let it start to set. Add to potato-beet mixture while still liquid. Season to taste with salt and pepper. Add vinegar, peanut oil and mustard. Add more salt and pepper if needed. Oil charlotte or flat bottom mold well. Fill with salad mixture. Refrigerate at least 2 hours. Longer is better. Combine mayonnaise and tomato paste. Cover and refrigerate.

   Shortly before serving time, unmold salad onto a round platter. Coat with tomato mayonnaise. Garnish the top of the salad with carrots. Stud mayonnaise with olive slices. Arrange small bouquets of watercress about the base. Sprinkle watercress with more olive slices. Makes 6 to 8 servings.

SALADE JURASSIENNE
Cauliflower Salad with Green Beans and Cheese

1 medium cauliflower
10 ozs. string beans
5 ozs. Gruyere cheese, thinly sliced
6 tbs. peanut oil
2 tbs. tarragon vinegar
salt and pepper
2 tsp. chopped chives
2 hard-cooked eggs
1 tbs. chopped parsley

Early in the day, cook the whole head of cauliflower in boiling, salted water 10 minutes. Cook beans according to the Paul Mayer Method on page 5. (If beans are large put them through a French slicer before cooking.) Drain and dry beans. Cut cheese into matchsticks. When cauliflower is cooked, drain and dry it thoroughly. Separate into cauliflowerettes. Place in the center of a round plate. Blend oil, vinegar, salt, pepper and chopped chives together well. Pour half of dressing over cauliflower. Combine string beans, cheese

and remaining dressing. Mix well. Finely chop eggs and mix with parsley. Sprinkle over cauliflower. Arrange small bouquets of the bean-cheese mixture around the cauliflower. Refrigerate.

About one half hour before serving time, remove salad from refrigerator. Serve cold but not chilled. Makes 6 servings.

SALADE ANTIBOISE AUX HARICOTS VERTS
Green Bean Salad with Garlic Mayonnaise

1 lb. fresh string beans
1 green pepper
1 sweet red pepper <u>or</u> 2 canned pimientos
4 ozs. pitted black olives
3 cloves garlic
1 sweet onion
1/2 tsp. basil
2 tbs. red wine vinegar
1 cup olive oil
yolk of a 7 minute egg
salt and pepper
1 small head chicory
4 tomatoes
3 hard-cooked eggs, quartered

160

Early in the day, wash and trim beans. French slice and then cut slices into 4 pieces. Cook beans according to the Paul Mayer Method on page 5. Immediately rinse with cold water, drain and dry. Wash and dry peppers. Cut in half and remove seeds. Slice into long thin strips. Drain and dry olives. Slice onion and separate slices into rings. Wrap in plastic and refrigerate. Wash chicory. Drain, dry and finely chop. Toss beans, peppers, olives and chicory together. Cover and refrigerate. Put garlic through a press and place in blender container. Add basil, vinegar, 2 tablespoons olive oil and egg yolk. Cover and blend 15 seconds. Remove cover and add remaining olive oil in thin stream, forcing oil into blades until mayonnaise thickens. Season with salt and pepper. Quarter 3 tomatoes and toss with chilled ingredients. Add mayonnaise and mix gently. Cover and refrigerate.

At serving time, slice remaining tomato and cut eggs into quarters. Garnish salad with tomato slices, egg quarters and onion slices. Makes 6 servings.

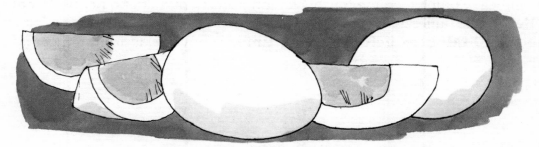

SALADE EMILIE
Fruit and Meat Salad with Mint Cream Dressing

6 small green apples
1 bunch celery
3 bananas
5 ozs. ham, julienned
5 ozs. tongue, julienned

6 large lettuce leaves
6 tbs. creme fraiche, page 4
juice of 1 small lemon
1 sprig mint, finely chopped
salt and pepper

162

In the very late afternoon, peel, core and quarter apples. Cut quarters into thin slices. Cut all the leaves and most of the stalks from celery. Slice celery heart the same way as apples. Peel bananas and thinly slice. Toss apples, celery and bananas together. Add ham and tongue and mix lightly. Line a small salad bowl with lettuce leaves. Arrange salad mixture on lettuce. Combine creme fraiche, lemon juice, mint, salt and pepper. Coat salad with sauce. Refrigerate until serving time.

About 10 minutes before serving time, remove salad from refrigerator. Makes 6 servings.

FILETS DE HARNEG HAMBOURGEOISE
Herring Salad Hamburg Style

3 cooked potatoes, diced
3 gherkins, finely chopped
2 ozs. onion, finely chopped
1/4 lb. cooked beets, diced
2 tbs. vinegar

6 tbs. olive oil
salt and pepper
2 hard-cooked eggs
6 fillets kippered herring (not canned)
4 tsp. chopped parsley

Early in the day, combine potatoes, gherkins, onions and beets in a large bowl. Add 163
vinegar, olive oil, salt and pepper. Mix thoroughly. Arrange salad on a round platter. Separate egg yolks from whites and put through a sieve separately. Cut herring into thin strips. Make a lattice of herring strips across the top of the salad. Fill the diamonds formed by the herring alternately with egg white, egg yolk and chopped parsley. Refrigerate.

A few minutes before needed, remove salad from refrigerator. Serve cold but not chilled. Makes 6 servings.

A BEAUTYFUL VISTA
FOR THOSE DRIVING THE
CORNICHE D'OR BETWEEN
ST. RAPHAEL AND CANNES

M. NELSON
74

DESSERTS

Everybody likes dessert, including the cook, because in many instances the work has been accomplished well before, and it takes only a trip to the kitchen and back to bring an already successful dinner party to a flamboyant and exciting conclusion.

Even hot desserts can be included in the do-it-ahead scheme of things, as some of the recipes included here demonstrate.

As I have mentioned earlier, a restaurateur acquaintance maintains that the beginning and ending of the meal are the most important, and I certainly cannot dispute the fact that what one eats for dessert is most often remembered and thought of as the highlight of the meal.

Therefore, it behooves the ambitious hostess not only to put her best foot forward throughout the entire dinner, but to take a giant step when dessert time comes. The following recipes are designed to put you way out front.

MOUSSE DE POMMES AU GRAND MARNIER
Apple Mousse with Custard Sauce

7/8 cup sugar
3 tbs. water
4 tbs. butter, melted
1 lb. green cooking apples
3/4 cup sugar
4 egg whites
3 tbs. Grand Marnier
Custard Sauce, page 167

Early in the day, combine sugar and water in small saucepan. Cook until sugar dissolves and barely turns golden. Pour into a 1-quart mold. Turn mold to coat sides completely. Set aside. Peel, core and thinly slice apples. Place in buttered, ovenproof dish. Pour butter over apples and mix until apples are coated. Cover with foil and bake in 350°F. oven 20 minutes. Run cooked apples through the fine blade of a meat grinder. Add 3/4-cup sugar. Place ground apples in a saucepan and shake over heat to drive out excess water. Refrigerate until chilled. **When apples are chilled,** beat egg whites until stiff. Fold into chilled apples along with Grand Marnier. Pour into coated mold. Set mold in pan of hot water. Bake 1 hour in 325°F. oven. Remove from oven and refrigerate. Prepare Custard Sauce. Thoroughly chill both mousse and sauce.

Just before serving time, unmold mousse. Coat with some of Custard Sauce. Pour remaining sauce into a bowl and pass separately. Makes 6 servings.

Custard Sauce

4 egg yolks
7/8 cup sugar
1-1/3 cups milk
1 tsp. vanilla

Combine egg yolks and sugar in top of double boiler. Beat until light and fluffy. Mix milk and vanilla in saucepan. Heat just to boiling point. Beat hot milk into egg mixture. Cook over hot water, stirring, until nicely thickened. Pour into bowl and refrigerate immediately.

PUDDING GRANDMERE
Bread Pudding with Apricot Sauce

Apricot Sauce, page 169
1/2 lb. currants
6 ozs. candied fruit
1 lb. stale bread
1 qt. milk

4 tbs. melted butter
9 tbs. sugar
4 eggs, beaten
4 tbs. rum

168

Early in the day, make apricot sauce so it can be chilling. **Early in the afternoon,** blanch currants and candied fruit. Dry and set aside. Break bread into crumbs. Combine crumbs and milk. Stir to a paste. Add melted butter, sugar, eggs, rum, currants and candied fruit. Stir until well mixed. Pour batter into a well-buttered, 9-inch springform pan. Bake in 350°F. oven 1 hour and 15 minutes, or until a knife inserted into center of pudding comes out clean. Remove from oven. Let stand at room temperature until serving time.

At serving time, unmold pudding onto serving plate. Serve with Chilled Apricot Sauce. Makes 6 servings.

Apricot Sauce

4 ozs. dried apricots*
1/2 cup sugar
2-1/4 cups water

   Combine apricots, sugar and water in deep saucepan. Bring to boil. Reduce heat and cook slowly 40 minutes. Pour into blender container. Cover and puree on high speed. Pour into bowl and chill until serving time.

*dried pears may be used instead of apricots, if desired.

LA DENTELLES MARTINIQUAISES
Coconut Cream Crepes with Rum Sauce

Crepes, page 171
Rum Sauce, page 171
Pastry Cream, page 172
4 bananas
4 tbs. butter

170

Early in the day, prepare crepes as directed. Stack cooked crepes on a plate. They will separate easier if not placed squarely on top of each other. It is not necessary to put waxed paper between each one. Cover tightly with plastic wrap and refrigerate. **In the afternoon,** make Rum Sauce and Pastry Cream as directed. Cover and refrigerate. **About an hour before serving time,** peel bananas and split in half lengthwise. Saute in foaming butter just until barely cooked. Spread each crepe with a spoonful of Pastry Cream. Place a cooked banana half on each crepe and roll up. Arrange stuffed crepes in a lightly buttered, ovenproof serving dish. Remove Rum Sauce from refrigerator.

Just before serving time, pour Rum Sauce over stuffed crepes. Place dish under broiler or in a hot oven only until sauce is nicely browned. Serve at once. Makes 8 servings.

Crepes

1 cup flour	1/4 cup sugar	4 tbs. melted butter
3 eggs	grated rind 2 oranges	6 tbs. milk
pinch of salt	grated rind 1 lemon	3 tbs. rum

Mix all ingredients together. Beat until smooth. Then add enough water to bring batter to the consistency of whipping cream. Using a 10-inch crepe pan or skillet, make 8 large crepes of equal size. Use as directed.

Rum Sauce

6 egg yolks	1/2 cup whipping cream	1/2 cup sugar
8 tbs. butter	1/2 tsp. arrowroot	1/2 cup rum

Combine egg yolks, butter, whipping cream, arrowroot, sugar and rum in a heavy saucepan or top of double boiler. Cook, stirring, over low to medium heat, or over hot water until sauce thickens. Use as directed.

Pastry Cream

1-1/2 cups grated coconut
2 cups milk
3/4 cup sugar
6 egg yolks
1/2 cup flour
1 tsp. vanilla

Combine coconut and milk in saucepan. Heat to just below the boiling point. Strain, squeezing coconut to extract all the flavor. Discard coconut. Combine sugar, egg yolks, flour and vanilla in saucepan. Beat until light and fluffy. Heat coconut milk and add to mixture. Stir vigorously as you add. Place over medium heat and continue stirring briskly until mixture just comes to boil. Pour into bowl and cover closely with plastic wrap to prevent skin from forming. Set aside.

GATEAU CHOCOLAT
Chocolate Cake

Several
days
ahead

3 eggs
1/2 cup sugar
4 ozs. bitter chocolate
8 tbs. butter
1 cup sifted cake flour
whipped cream

173

As far as 8 days ahead, cream eggs and sugar together until light and fluffy. Melt chocolate and butter together. Beat into creamed mixture. Add flour and mix well. Turn into small, well-buttered mold or springform pan. Bake in 325°F. oven 50 minutes. Remove from pan. Wrap tightly and store in tin box.

At serving time, cut into small pieces. Serve on dessert plates with whipped cream on the side. Makes 6 servings.

GATEAU MOUSSELINE
Sponge Cake with Chocolate Sauce

3 ozs. raisins
8 eggs
1-1/8 cups sugar
1 tsp. vanilla
1 cup sifted cake flour
4 ozs. potato flour
Creme Anglaise Chocolat, page 175

174

Early in the day, blanch and dry raisins. Set aside. Separate eggs. Beat egg yolks until very thick. Gradually add sugar. Beat until mixture is thick. Add vanilla and continue beating until mixture is pale and very thick. Gradually add cake flour by sifting a little at a time over egg mixture. Fold in gently. Sift potato flour over batter and gently fold it in until all is mixed. Beat egg whites until stiff but not dry. Carefully fold into batter along with raisins. Pour batter into a buttered 9-inch springform pan. Bake in 350°F. oven 1 hour or until straw comes out clean when inserted into center of cake. (Cake may take longer than 1 hour, so rely on test more than the timing.) Cool cake slightly, then remove from form. Cool. Cover lightly until needed. **While cake is baking,** prepare sauce and refrigerate until serving time.

   To serve, place slices of cake on dessert plates. Spoon chilled sauce over cake. Makes 6 servings.

Creme Anglaise Chocolat

2 cups milk
1/2 cup <u>plus</u> 2 tbs. sugar
1/2 oz. potato flour
3-1/2 ozs. bitter chocolate
6 egg yolks

   Combine all ingredients together in top of double boiler. Cook over hot water until mixture thickens. Remove at once from hot water. Pour into bowl and refrigerate until well chilled. Serve spooned over cake.

TARTE AU CHOCOLAT
Chocolate Tart

1-3/4 cups sifted flour
1/4 tsp. salt
7 tbs. butter
3 tbs. cold water

7 ozs. semi-sweet chocolate
2 tbs. water
3/4 cup creme fraiche, page 4
2 ozs. peeled pistachios, chopped

The day before, combine flour and salt in mixing bowl. Cut butter into flour with pastry blender until mixture resembles fine meal. Sprinkle with water and mix by tossing lightly with a fork until dough gathers into a ball. Allow dough to rest 1 hour. Then roll dough out and line an 8-inch tart pan or flan ring. Prick pastry all over with a fork. Bake in 350ºF. oven 20 minutes. Remove from oven and chill. **While tart shell is chilling,** melt chocolate in saucepan with 2 tablespoons of water. Add creme fraiche. Fill tart shell with chocolate mixture. Refrigerate overnight.

To serve, decorate the top of tart with chopped pistachios. Cut into wedges and serve on dessert plates. Makes 6 servings.

TARTE AUX POIRES
Pear Tart

1-3/4 cups sifted flour
1/4 tsp. salt
7 tbs. butter
3 tbs. ice water
5 tbs. sugar

1-1/4 lbs. pears
1 egg
1 tbs. flour
2 tbs. melted butter
2 tbs. rum

Early in the afternoon, combine flour and salt in mixing bowl. Cut butter into flour until mixture is coarse and crumbly. Sprinkle with water. Mix by tossing gently with fork until dough gathers into a ball. Set aside for 1 hour. Then roll out and line an 8-inch tart pan or flan ring. Sprinkle pastry with 2 tablespoons sugar. Peel and core pears. Cut each pear into 6 lengthwise slices. Neatly arrange slices in pastry-lined pan. Combine egg, remaining 3 tablespoons sugar, flour, butter and rum. Pour over pears. Bake in 350°F. oven 30 minutes. Remove from oven and cool at room temperature until serving time.

To serve, cut tart into wedges and serve on dessert plates. Makes 6 servings.

177

TARTE ALSACIENNE
Plum Tart

1-3/4 cups flour	1 egg yolk
1/4 tsp. salt	6 tbs. creme fraiche, page 4
7 tbs. butter	5 tbs. sugar
3 tbs. ice water	2 tbs. flour
2-1/4 lbs. small blue plums	2 tbs. Kirsch
1 egg	

178

Early in the day, combine flour and salt in mixing bowl. Cut in butter with pastry blender until mixture resembles fine meal. Sprinkle water over mixture and blend by tossing lightly with a fork until dough gathers into a ball. Allow dough to rest 1 hour. Roll dough out and line a 9-inch tart pan or flan ring with the pastry. Refrigerate. **About 2 hours before serving time,** cut plums in half lengthwise and remove pits. Arrange plum halves in a crown pattern in the unbaked tart shell. Beat egg, egg yolk, creme fraiche, sugar, flour and Kirsch together. Pour over plums. Bake tart in 350°F. oven 35 minutes or until filling has set and browned. Remove from oven and cool at room temperature.

To serve, cut into wedges and serve on dessert plates. Makes 6 servings.

BAVAROISE AUX PRUNEAUX
Prune Bavarian Cream

One day ahead

2 cups water
1 lb. pitted prunes
3 tbs. sugar
grated rind of 1 lemon
1 pkg. (1 tbs.) unflavored gelatine
2 ozs. blanched candied fruit
1 cup (1/2 pt.) cream, whipped
candied fruit for garnish

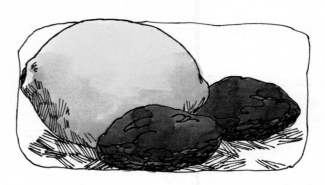

179

The night before or early in the day, bring 2 cups water to boil in medium saucepan. Add prunes, sugar and lemon rind. Reduce heat. Cover and simmer over low heat 1 hour. Soften gelatine in 1/2-cup cold water. Add to prunes 5 minutes before cooking time is completed. Transfer to large mixer bowl and beat until everything has been mashed and blended. Blanch and dry candied fruit. Add to prunes. Oil an attractive mold. Fill with prune mixture. Cover and refrigerate overnight, or at least 2 hours.

At serving time, unmold dessert onto an attractive serving plate. Decorate with whipped cream and candied fruit. Pass extra whipped cream in a bowl. Makes 6 servings.

INDEX